Nemesis

By

David Brown

ISBN 978-1-907629-26-6

MMXI

Published by
ShieldCrest
Aylesbury, Buckinghamshire, HP22 5RR
England
www.shieldcrest.co.uk

CONTENTS

PROLOGUE

Screams & shrieks echoed across the desolate Suffolk countryside. The grey & dripping November dawn had come and gone. The two children had left for nursery school and all had been quiet and peaceful until ten o'clock had struck on the grandfather clock in the small hall of the cottage. It was the morning of Thursday 19th November 1963. The pretty Hope Cottage at the base of Bell Hill stood quietly with its single companion as it had done for some 60 years. The lane climbed gently up the low hill to the Bell Inn; once the haunt of smugglers and now of members of CAMRA and lovers of real ale.

What was the cause of the commotion coming from the little grey cottage at the base of the hill? A passer-by entering the front gate and crossing the lawn to the left hand sitting room window would have witnessed a strange scene within. A tallish well-built sandy haired man stood over an auburn haired woman, who was sitting at a desk facing the window, his powerful hands around her throat. Her face was distorted with pain as the last screams of life were wrenched from her struggling body. At the same time an elderly fat lady was beating the man furiously with a wicker shopping basket and shrieking at the top of her voice.

When it was all over the police were called and the children were collected and taken far away to a house in Northampton which they had known before where various children were living & were looked after by a former school companion of the victim.

Later that day as the diesel train from Marylebone drifted lazily along just before Rickmansworth station, David who had devoured most of the evening paper and was perusing the stop press came up with a start. The headline Murder in Suffolk was of minor interest only but the details of the victim & the attacker brought tears to his eyes & anguish to his heart. As he said to his wife Audrey as he arrived home in Rickmansworth a short walk from the station. Those poor children we shall have to do something!

On a slightly later train his younger brother Rupert read the very same report and said to his Father as he arrived home in Amersham, what is going to happen to those poor children? Thus the scene is set for the harrowing true tale which had started so happily some thirty five years before and would end so sadly some 45 years later.

≈ 1 ≈

A Bright Dawn

The story begins happily in 1930 in a maternity home in Bishops Stortford where the fat lady Margaret is giving birth to her first and only child the product of a marriage of a few years earlier made not in the first bloom of life, to a dapper middle aged dairy farmer of forty five years with a full head of grey hair.

They lived nearby in a grand Victorian mansion with its accompanying small farm which was owned by a Cambridge College. This struggling farmer was building up a small herd of pedigree Guernsey cattle with an associated small retail milk business attached. The house had an impressive if somewhat rutted drive, a large peaceful rose garden with many specimen rose bushes with a distant view of the local church. It also had a fabulous kitchen garden and this, along with the rose garden, was the farmer, Tom Brown's, pride and joy. This garden was the source of much rich produce as each fruit and vegetable came into season. The gardening interest was the result of Tom's initial trade, starting as a gardener in the local big house, some thirty years previously and rising to head gardener until this progress was rudely interrupted by war service in the First World War. As an older man with management experience Tom was recommended for WOSBE and rose to the rank of Captain in the horse artillery. He asked his younger brother Sydney then a Sergeant Major why he did not do likewise and apply for WOSBE to which Sydney sagely replied; 'Because I don't want to be shot in the front or the back'.

The baby was brought back home & Fiona began her closeted, happy & privileged upbringing which she so bitterly regretted in later life as life grew harder. At the age of four the first of many ponies a tiny Shetland name Sue was acquired. She was followed by many ever larger and more expensive successors. At this time began the regular Pony Club events at the farm becoming a regular feature of the local social calendar. At these events Captain Tom and his wife Margaret would stroll around offering encouragement to children, parents and organisers alike. At an early stage a faithful nanny was engaged and this was followed by a succession of expensive private schools and finally a well-known finishing school at Winkfield, which included a period in Switzerland. Fiona was a healthy girl apart from persistent slight asthma although, like her Mother, she was rather heavily built.

As Fiona grew up her riding skills had advanced leading eventually to public show jumping. Even in the early 1950's appearances at the Horse of the Year Show on TV, inclusion in the British show jumping team and in the social calendar of the fashionable press. During these latter years the farm was visited on summer Sundays by Tom's brother Sydney his wife Doris and their two sons David and Rupert. Like Captain Tom Sydney the younger brother by about three years had married late in life at the age of 47 in 1934. The arrival of their offspring was somewhat slow but in November 1937 David was born after a somewhat anguished period and very prematurely. Finally in January 1943 his younger brother Rupert was born. These boys also spent holidays at the farm, especially after they attended Public School, as this attendance assisted Margaret in her ever active social climbing.

All this social excitement was nothing when Fiona faced the need to earn a living to support herself and her children if she could not bear her married life any longer. As she said to her much loved Aunt Margaret shortly before her death; 'If only my Father had brought me up to earn a living rather than to be a Lady'. However ,we must not rush ahead too fast for in the dawn of life all seems fresh and bright, hardships are small and the future beckons with existing hope.

Even as late as the early 1950's and without an expensive presentation at court a furious dredging of the marriage market could be conducted by an ambitious Mother. Thus the ever socially aggressive Margaret conducted with ruthless, if misguided, and erratic energy. Soon a series of well-known young men, some of dubious character, were invited to the farm to partake of delicious meals prepared in the vast kitchen and served in the impressively large dining room with its huge solid oak furniture.

Finally in 1954 a sandy haired scot appeared, Morris Macpherson. Although not quite to the social standard Margaret had sought for her daughter, he had an impressive job with excellent prospects and was highly ambitious. Designated a high flyer in spite of a failed degree he worked for a major company operating in Africa and throughout the world. An engagement was announced and an excited Margaret telephoned her brother in law Sydney to tell the good news and its precipitate cause. Fiona was to become engaged to Morris and a wedding would take place in the British Embassy in Leopoldville upon arrival in the Belgian Congo where married life would begin. Before this a grand family engagement party would be held at the farm to celebrate the occasion. The cynical Sydney was not impressed. Although careful not to reveal the full details of the situation;

'That stupid woman he raged. I would not rejoice at the ruination of my only daughter!'

So it was on a late March day in 1954 members of the family assembled at the farm. The whisky flowed in the smallish library with its roaring log fire where one could sit on the sofa facing the flames as warm as toast while ones back was icy cold. There was no such thing as central heating in that house at that time. Copious drinks were served and nibbles were provided. David drank his first glass of whisky, albeit a chotapeg heavily diluted with water. This was the first of many in later life, having ascertained that cider was not available, and not yet having developed his later taste for beer. After this they all moved into the impressive dining room where a dry white wine was served with the prawn cocktail starter. This was followed by roast lamb with roast potatoes onion sauce, leeks, mashed swede and sprouts. Almost all the vegetables were from the copious kitchen garden. All was washed down with a fine claret.

Then a shivering Charlotte Russe was served with cream from the dairy and finally coffee with more cream, mints and liqueurs, where mainly Drambuie was chosen. David found the sweetness of Drambuie was then much more suited to his taste than the harsher whisky even if it was generously diluted with water.

After this heavy meal the two farming brothers and the younger members of the family, including the happy couple, walking some distance behind, strolled round the grounds as was customary on Sydney's visits. This started with the walled vegetable garden with its seed beds ready for the coming years produce. Obviously the now 69 year old Captain Tom could no longer be the major labourer in this considerable enterprise and discussion began on the excellent work of John the youngish gardener who was responsible under Captain Tom's experienced guidance. The amount of the dairy herd's by-product of well-rotted compost was remarked upon, as were the soft fruit beds. The garden was dotted with a number of apple, plum and peach trees the latter growing against the sunniest walls. The small number of pear trees were about to break into their short and early spring blossoms. Finally the condition of the herd of pedigree Guernsey cattle was admired subject to Sydney's expert eye. As always the tour excluded the dairy itself while in the distance across the fields the lights of Bishops Stortford twinkled in the gathering dusk and the bells of the parish church began ringing to welcome the congregation to evensong.

Perhaps the only hint of the future storms which lay ahead of this happy occasion was the considerable quantity of whisky young Morris consumed and his constant smoking of cigarettes, although at that time this was not often thought to be harmful in spite of the late Kings recent death and the growing claims of harm by the more advanced members of the medical profession. Indeed, as Sydney was fond of recalling, as an ardent reformed ex-smoker, when he remarked upon his GP being caught smoking at a Rotary lunch, the culprit had said; 'Well you have got to have something to kill you.' This was typical of the relaxed approach to this vice in those times.

In Sydney and Doris's Morris Cowley on the way home with David and Rupert in the back, the conversation was about the excellence of the meal and the erratic nature of the heating. Also the poor conversation of Margaret with her constant harping about grand connections and the state of the toilet pans, a particular observation of Doris whose own toilets were sparkling! These reflections over the event were mundane and revealed no inkling of oncoming problems.

After the party the happy couple went on a month's holiday in Malta. They were able to throw themselves into the social whirl of the many British residents associated with the great naval base of that time. While strolling round the street market many items of delicate linen were bargained for. In the evenings cocktail parties and dances were attended. Fiona was especially horrified at the many stories of priestly conceived bastards amongst the local inhabitants. Of course this was long before the current exposure of the monstrous iniquities of the Catholic Church in the areas of sexual conduct.

≈ 2 ≈

Advance to Africa

The gathering of huts at the end of the runway known as London Airport North, in spite of its ramshackle appearance, still gave the impression that airline passengers were important and had some status. The endless queues and cattle herding of recent years were not a feature with such a small number of passengers. The flight was as usual delayed and the happy couple consumed a full bottle of champagne before boarding. During the flight passengers were allowed to smoke and complementary alcohol was served to ease the discomfort of the cramped seating and excessive engine noise. Both Morris and Fiona took full advantage of these facilities. The cramped airline seating presented an increasing source of discomfort for Fiona although she relished the splendid meals provided with the continuous flow of champagne.

Upon arrival the stark conditions of the airport with its crowd of excited native porters in the early morning after only fitful sleep made London Airport North seem a sumptuous memory. Upon leaving the plane the atmosphere struck like entering a sauna. In spite of the workers standing around the baggage area some passengers climbed the barriers and struggled with their own luggage carrying it out to the waiting taxis. This was impossible for Morris and Fiona with their copious baggage including her mother's carefully packed trousseau with household linen as well as much clothing and cosmetics. Morris had warned that such items would be hard to come by and expensive in the Congolese shops. At last a couple of porters were engaged and the party and luggage moved outside to a waiting taxi. The taxi was without air conditioning and after time consuming loading was driven very erratically along the long road into Leopoldville. In spite of the early hour in the sweaty heat hundreds of people were already walking into town on their way to work. Some had heavy loads and staggered into or across the road narrowly avoiding disaster from the speeding but sparse traffic. This led to violent evasive actions on the part of the taxi driver. It is not surprising under these conditions that Fiona began to feel unwell. As they approached the centre of town the tall concrete buildings appeared to touch the lowering clouds that hung over the city and even at this early hour the air was completely stifling after the coolness of the plane.

Arrival at the hotel was a little more civilised, a smartly dressed Baluba was summoning smaller Luala to seize bags and rush them into reception where they were piled in a jumbled heap. The Hotel Royale had an air of faded grandure which reflected the already collapsing Belgian hold over their massive Congolese Colony. The air conditioning, while effective when switched on, emitted an ominous cloud of yellow dust while starting up. After a refreshingly pleasant breakfast, Morris felt much better and the couple returned to their room for an affectionate siesta and a lengthy much needed sleep. On awakening, they were unpacking and preparing their outfits for the wedding ceremony at the British embassy for the next week, when Fiona, who had eaten and drank very little, began to suffer a massive asthma attack. Soon a Doctor was called who called for immediate hospitalisation. As a result she was carried off to the nearest hospital where she was kept for some weeks. This all started a lengthy period of illness followed by several months convalescence. Thus it was approaching Christmas before Morris collected Fiona and took her to the comfortable accommodation in Stanleyville provided by the company. A few months later, early in 1955, a quiet wedding ceremony took place at the local Baptist Mission station. A kindly elderly couple ran it and provided schooling for the local population. In the months following, Fiona's health continued to be a source of problems. Finally in early July 1957 Fiona again became pregnant.

This was the time when Professor A J von Belsen produced his paper 'A 50 year plan for the emancipation of Belgian Africa.' This was supported by the Catholic Church and planned for the emergence of a nation with Europeans and Africans on an equal footing. However it was far too late for that. This plan was opposed by Abako a political party led by Joseph Kasavubu who was demanding immediate independence. A rash of tribal groupings was opposing the artificial unity of the vast territory. A new Belgian Government was formed and declared a policy of decolonisation. This was encouraged by the meddling United Nations and the rivalry of the two top dog nations. The USA with its foolhardy obsession with decolonisation resulting from its cathartic experience of repudiating the so called British Colonial yoke some 171 years previously and the Soviet Union with its worldwide Communist objectives. These objectives stretched into the Congo itself in the shape of the communist Patrice Lumumba and his party the Movement Nationale Congolais the only party claiming a national outreach. In the meantime in Katanga close to the home of Morris and Fiona, Moise Tshombie formed the more moderate Conokat with its links and borders alongside the powerful British controlled Northern and Southern Rhodesia with its then nearly born Central African Federation, which was so soon to be destroyed by the wicked outside forces so cruelly creating the mayhem and disaster of the Congo which continues even to the present day.

Against this back ground life in Stanleyville continued in a safe and more serene path. Both Morris and Fiona were partaking rather too much of the relief provided to the white man's burden by alcohol in spite of Fiona's pregnancy. They threw themselves vigorously into the social whirl of cocktail and swimming parties. Fortunately, this did not affect the pregnancy and on the 31st of March 1958 a daughter, Anne, was born in Stanleyville. It was clear from the start of her life that Anne was a sickly child who was not thriving. Obscure problems were diagnosed and obscure treatments undertaken culminating in a six months stay in hospital where steroids and powerful antibiotics were given. Finally Anne returned to her home in September of that year. Fiona was of course unused to having her social life interrupted by the needs of a young baby, so the first of a series of amahs or nannies was engaged. In October and November of that year Margaret visited from England for some six weeks. The hot damp climate did not suit Northern Europeans especially those who were more solidly built. As a result Fiona found her Mothers attentions were of little help with the baby. Margaret of course revelled in the attentions of the Congolese servants and sat in the shade of the impressive villa grounds sipping tea and watching the children playing with the native amahs in the shade or lying languidly in their prams while their Mothers made polite and stilted conversation. They occasionally alluded to the horrors that were moving ever closer. However as Margaret declared in the telephone call to Sydney on her return to England the troubles were a long way away and their lives were untouched by these rumours.

In 1958 a conference of Independent African Peoples was held in Accra Ghana. Kasavubu was not allowed to attend but Lumumba was and returned inspired by Nkrumah's ideas and policies and petulantly claimed independence at once. This was of course before the local Ghanian population wisely allowed Flight Lieutenant Rawlings the son of a Scottish missionary and a local lady to seize power and create a haven of peace and prosperity that looks set to endure. Almost alone among African leaders this wise man has relinquished power and in retirement continues to provide wise and civilised counsel to his people without any apparent corruption, greed or self-aggrandisement. Following Lumumba's declaration, agitation and unemployment caused riots, arson and bloodshed in Leopoldville in January1959. In the next month, before Anne was even a year old, Fiona again became pregnant and so a second daughter Freda was born in Stanleyville on the 25th November 1959. Although smaller in frame than Anne, Freda took after her wiry Scottish Grandmother. In this respect, she was tougher than Anne and her difficulties after birth were not so great.

In January 1960 the Belgian Government convened a round table conference in Brussels and representatives of all political parties and Congolese chiefs attended. Everyone agreed immediate independence for 30th June 1960. This was in response to lunatic pressure from the UN, the USA and the Soviet Union. The proposed constitution was a cause of dispute. The MNC wanted centralisation but this was opposed by most of the other Congolese parties including Abako though it was favoured by the Belgians and the Chiefs. Finally centralisation was accepted as a temporary starting point. Fortunately at this time the company decided to move Morris and his young family to the comparative safety of Kenya. Clearly the oncoming independence was going to be a total disaster and the Congo was going to become an even more unsuitable place for a young family.

≈ 3 ≈

The Calm before the Storm

After flying to Nairobi the family travelled by road through Nyeri to the white highlands where the comfortable company villa lay surrounded by fields. Anne had been very upset to leave her Congolese amah with whom she had a very strong relationship. As she said in later life; 'My parents were fancy people and they were not interested in us children.' So such a relationship was vitally important to her. However, she soon settled with her warm and kindly ever present Bantu replacement and life for the whole family was much more relaxed and happy in the better climate and with the more civilised background of a British administration.

The Mau Mau emergency which had been declared in 1952 was largely over although mopping up operations were still in evidence in their area. Anne vividly later recalled seeing the surrounding fields full of troops with guns. During the early summer Fiona and the children had a short holiday at the farm back in England. The visit beginning in early June coincided with a period of glorious weather. During the visit Fiona's godmother Aunt Margaret came down from London with the two friends that she usually brought with her on one of her customary raids on the vegetable garden as Captain

Tom used to describe it. After a pleasant but busy visit all three returned laden with bags and baskets full of produce. During this holiday as a result of the good weather much time was spent in the sun in the rose garden. Anne remembered her Grandfather's fury when he discovered she had destroyed all the blooms on his favourite rose. This anger was doubtless strengthened by the fact that Fiona and Margaret were sitting chatting nearby clearly oblivious to Anne's activities beside Freda kicking in her pram. Maybe his excessive anger was a sign of his declining health. Later in the autumn he was suddenly rushed to hospital with a mysterious virus which was ascribed to removing ragwort from one of his fields. This pretty weed is well known amongst horse owners as highly poisonous to horses. By this time the young family had returned to Kenya where life continued peacefully and happily.

Both Morris and Fiona found the social life of this area of Kenya much to their liking and they were able to throw themselves into this with enormous energy and enjoyment as a result of their native servants. This meant that the children were left more and more with their native amah. It is not surprising that a very devoted relationship grew up between the amah and the older Anne. This pleasant and happy interlude was to be brutally and suddenly brought to an end.

At the beginning of April of the following year back in Amersham in England, David married his long time fiancée Audrey. Captain Tom and Margaret declined to attend without any reason being given but a present was sent. Then suddenly on the 8th April 1961 Captain Tom collapsed and died at the farm having suffered a sudden Coronary Thrombosis at the age of 76. In spite of their 14 year age difference Margaret was devastated and completely fell to pieces. She was just about able to telephone her Daughter Fiona in Kenya with the sad news. As a result the whole family returned to England almost immediately and the company, after granting Morris three months compassionate leave, decided that Morris should eventually return to a new posting in British Guyana. Obviously he would initially be on his own and the rest of the family would follow on. It was clearly going to take a considerable time for Fiona to help her Mother to sell up the farm and find a new home.

Thus, for a second time Anne was to find that a very close relationship with a beloved amah had suddenly ended. It was David's later belief with hind sight that she was never to recover from this. It is a widely recognised fact that young children form very close and important relationships with substitute mother figures. Because of this it has been possible for families who have been living abroad to sponsor nannies as essential UK workers so bringing them back with them. This was provided that they had acted as a nanny for more than two years. Of course in this case this latter condition did not apply.

The funeral had to be delayed until the family had packed up permanently and returned to the farm. Thus it was in the last week of the month that a funeral was held at 3 pm at the local church within sight of the rose garden at the farm. In spite of it being nearly May the weather was very cold and wet and overcoats were much favoured by the considerable congregation. This was followed by a cremation at the local crematorium which was some distance away. Sydney had driven over from Amersham with his younger brother Stanley after picking him up from the original family farm, the home of their long dead parents. David came down on the train from work in London intending to drive them back. After the cremation ceremony it was decided that they would not return to the farm for the wake as everyone was tired and the crematorium was close to their route home. Thus they did not meet the children who were with the daily help back at the farm.

David drove straight back to his little house in Rickmansworth where he now lived with his new wife. After a refreshing cup of tea Sydney took his brother back to the original family farm. The local pub, the White Horse at the corner of the lane leading to the farm drive, stood largely unchanged from when it was the scene of so much of their social life after the horrors of the First World War. This was where both Sydney and Tom had courted Margaret who lived nearby. Sydney later returned to his home in Amersham on his own where Rupert, on his return from work, waited to hear how the day had turned out. Tom's elder sisters had also not attended the funeral as the old fashioned belief that funerals were primarily the business of senior male members of the family seemed to still prevail in that old fashioned family.

Thus Captain Tom's favourite sister Aunt Margaret did not attend. The sister he had regularly visited in her small flat in Pimlico when he was on his regular lunches and visits to the Farmers Club. During these visits he had helped her with her financial affairs. He also came round when he had attended the annual member's days at the nearby Chelsea Flower Shows in the grounds of the Royal Hospital as well as shows in the horticultural halls in nearby Victoria. After starting work in London in May 1959 at the end of his National Service, David had also started to visit his favourite Aunt on one weekday evening after work. As a result he was able to give full details of the funeral and she asked him if he would help her with her affairs as her favourite brother had previously done. This was especially necessary because of her failing sight.

After the funeral there was much to be done. Captain Tom had left all his belongings on trust to his daughter Fiona with a life interest for his wife Margaret. His brother Sydney was fully aware of all the details as he was one of the executors. The farm, its contents, the animals and business all had to be disposed of. In addition while Morris was still in England it was agreed a joint home for Margaret and a base for the family should be acquired using the proceeds and a mortgage shared between Fiona and Morris. Sydney was very shocked to learn that the total proceeds from Tom's estate were only some £12,000. He felt this was very small in relation to his own resources especially bearing in mind the life style his brother and his wife had lead. A frantic search for a home was undertaken before Morris had left for George Town where he was now to be working. This was when the cottage at the base of Bell Hill in Suffolk close to the sea and some 30 mile from the farm had been chosen. This pretty cottage had stood beside its companion for some 100 years and had a surprisingly large garden with a small shallow lily pond in which the children subsequently played with the little boy from the next door cottage. One strange feature of the cottage was the fact that the garage was in a small field across the lane; this garage and field were included in the sale. Fiona had hoped to use this field for a pony for the girls. Margaret used this garage for her second hand Morris Minor which she had acquired after her husband's death and the disposal of their ancient Jowett Javelin. Captain Tom like his younger brother Stanley had never learned to drive and had relied on his wife to chauffeur him around.

Many of the larger pieces of furniture were much too large for the cottage's smaller rooms and had to be sold. The large oak dining room furniture with its massive sideboard, the table and chairs had to go. The matching oak tea trolley with its detachable tray was retained for sentimental reasons and provided an occasional table against the wall. This was useful for serving drinks with a lower shelf for a copious number of bottles this eventually became a table for a sound reproduction system. The very large Sofa and easy chairs from the seldom used drawing room were also disposed of. The smaller library furniture was retained. Morris supplied some of the smaller items from his old flat in Edinburgh which had been stored in the meantime by his Mother.

Fiona and the children stayed in England while all this was completed. So that it was October before they flew to the USA and then undertook the much shorter flight to join Morris in George Town. He had in the meantime worked and lived on his own in the comfortable and prestigious company villa. It was not surprising that in the small social circle of George Town at that time that he should meet the Prime minister of the colony Dr Chedi Jagen a Marxist of Indian descent. A number of meetings ensued at which Morris used his memories of the chaos the Marxists had caused in the Congo to discuss the progress of government in the colony as it moved towards independence. The country eventually achieved independence under the rule of Forbes Burnham an autocrat formerly a co-leader with Chedi Jagen but they had quarrelled. Forbes Burnham was greatly favoured by the USA because he was not a Marxist. Following his death after 21 years rule, Chedi Jagen became a distinguished leader of this small and poor country. While he was on his own Morris drank malt whisky in ever more copious quantities. When Fiona and the children joined him it was clear that he was far from well mentally and his subsequent breakdown led to a diagnosis of Manic Depression and to repatriation to England in September 1962 where treatment at a mental home in Northampton was prescribed. While he attended the mental home Fiona and the children stayed with an old school friend Diana nearby. This friend ran a small children's home with a number of animals a pony two dogs as well as hens, two cats, rabbits a hamster and a donkey. This strange world fascinated the children and to some extent relaxed the constant upheaval of their lives.

After six months treatment Morris was declared cured and the family all returned to the cottage in Suffolk where Margaret was a permanent resident. The harsh winter of that year lead to many limits on the lives of the inhabitants of the cottage including preventing Sydney David and Rupert visiting one Sunday in March due to a sudden heavy fall of snow which made the roads impassable. Accordingly the visit was postponed and everyone returned to their busy daily activities with no further communication until the end of the year and its dramatic events. The children were enrolled in the local nursery school and spent time playing with the little boy next door who recalled this many years later. At this time on one of his visits to Aunt Margaret, David heard she had been visited by Fiona Anne and Freda. She had produced in her inimitable way her usual sumptuous high tea which magically appeared without notice in spite of her living on her own in a small cramped flat. This was served on her antique 'Honiton' bone china with its pretty red and gold pattern scattered with red roses. She surprised David with the comment that she did not know who was the untidiest of the three, Fiona or one of the children.

At this time there was a curious incident with Anne, who was suddenly heard screaming and Morris was found with his hands round her neck. He claimed to be playing around but Margaret was not sure and Fiona was even more doubtful. Other warning signs were the large consumption of cheap whisky [life was more constrained in England] until the morning of 20th November dawned and Fiona informed Morris that she wished to obtain a divorce as living with him was too much of a strain for her and the children.

≈ 4 ≈

After Nemesis

On the Saturday of the last week of November the funeral was held in the church near to the now demolished farm, which has subsequently been replaced by a council estate. The only memory of the old farm is the names of two roads, Court and Manor roads. Apart from the road signs, there was nothing to indicate the farm had ever existed when David subsequently visited to travel from the newly built adjacent airport of Stansted. Without the considerable congregation of Captain Tom's funeral the church seemed to be barn like. The congregation was limited to Margaret her sole faithful friend Felicity, Audrey and David and the undertaker's men.

Audrey and David had travelled across country from their semidetached house in Rickmansworth their little newly acquired Austin A35. They had stopped in Harlow in a shopping area to buy some mushrooms for their Sunday breakfast. The parking restrictions were confusing stating that parking was only allowed on alternate sides of the road on the days Monday to Saturday. The signs stupidly did not indicate to which day each side applied. Since there was parking on both sides it was not clear on which side they should or should not park. Hence when they returned with the mushrooms there was a ticket placed prominently on the windscreen. David later disputed the ticket stating truthfully the circumstances of the visit and the purpose of the journey and that he had never visited the town before and was not likely to do so again. The ticket was rescinded, the authorities clearly presenting a more humane face then than they do today.

The service was a desperate and miserable affair the organ played gloomily at times but the service was entirely spoken and the vicar appeared anxious to reach the end in the shortest possible time. Margaret presented a pathetic spectacle dressed in a dirty and tattered mink coat, shaking with emotion from head to foot, wracked with sobs and presenting a most unpleasant smell which appeared to be caused by not washing since the recent tragedy. Felicity, her one faithful friend was kindly and smartly dressed as always, if a little horsey in appearance. Margaret had been taken to her nearby farm and stables shortly after the tragedy. After the brief service the coffin was taken through the old dripping churchyard to the new cemetery across the road. There, in the dripping drizzle, it was interred in a grave which was to remain unmarked for many years. It was from Felicity's farm that Margaret had phoned to report what Audrey and David already knew, and he had responded with his unshakable offer on behalf of himself and his wife to become responsible as parents for Anne and Freda by providing adoption, which was agreed. During the time at the farmhouse, over a delicious but miserable tea, the background to the tragedy was extensively discussed as of course the history of the past year was largely unknown to Audrey and David. Their offer was repeated and the phone number of the personnel manager of Morris's employer was handed over. It was he who had arranged for the children to be collected from nursery school and driven to Northampton to stay at the house where they had previously stayed with their Mother. Fiona's friend, Diana, was prepared to look after the children temporarily but not permanently. Margaret was clearly not capable of looking after herself let alone the children so it was not surprising that the company had been called upon to act in 'loco parentis'. The children's Scottish grandmother had stated that she wished to leave all care in Margaret's hands in view of what had happened. Whether she realised that these hands were totally incapacitated by the tragedy is not known. Audrey and David had never had any contact with Morris's family so they could not really get involved with this. For a short time after taking on the children David had corresponded with Mrs Macpherson but this contact stopped very quickly in part because he had so little spare time to do this and didn't feel able to undertake this task. In any case, the great distance between them was an enormous barrier to any contact. No interest was taken by any others of the Macpherson family with whom there had never been any contact. In addition, Margaret was not in any way close with Morris's family and almost certainly they had never met. No doubt Mrs Macpherson was so distraught that she could not bear to get any more involved and in any case with her social climbing, Margaret would have kept them at arm's length and out of sight.

As Audrey and David left, Felicity approached the car and began to say the things that she could not say in Margaret's presence. Firstly she stated that Margaret did not realise that she could never live with the children again. This seemed hard but true. She also said the awful words; 'You know he tried on Anne some three weeks before and was stopped by Fiona.' This lead in David's mind to a strengthening of his unshakeable conclusion that to protect the children and even his wife, Audrey, a no contact rule was vital even though contact seemed unlikely to be possible until a considerable time was passed. On the return home there was much to discuss and these discussions continued when

Rupert and Sydney came over for their customary Sunday lunch. Sydney was a little doubtful due to the size of the undertaking proposed. However he pursued his usual kindly acceptance of whatever the younger generation proposed. Rupert was as he remained for the rest of his life strongly approving and began a lifelong support of the enterprise doing everything possible to help and behaving in every way as an exemplary Uncle. It is interesting to reflect why both brothers were so united in their view that it was vital to welcome the children into the family. Both brothers had lost their Mother only fifty one months previously and both shared a sincere Christian belief arising from their strong Christian upbringing. In Rupert's case this still applies although David now totally rejects all religion as harmful. This is based upon his total conviction that there is no evidence what so ever that a good god exists and he prefers not to believe in an evil god. His previous beliefs have been replaced by the belief that mankind is subject to a vicious malicious and capricious fate. Audrey shared a Christian upbringing and belief which has endured, although she has since become a converted Roman Catholic.

Rupert and Sydney left early so that Audrey and David could visit Mary and Frederick, Audrey's parents, for tea and further intensive discussions. They were both very doubtful warning of the dangers at taking on two obviously disturbed children. This was the last time they were ever to make any unfavourable comment and they became the most devoted of adoptive grandparents. Of the senior members of the family, when David next visited, Aunt Margaret alone made no unfavourable comment and supported the situation for the rest of her life. This might have been expected as she was also Fiona's godmother.

On the following Monday morning David telephoned the number he had been given and spoke to Mr Shade the personnel manager. An appointment was made for next day at the company's impressive London offices for 2 pm. David travelled easily by tube in his lunch hour from the major computer company where he worked and the meeting started promptly. Mr Shade revealed that he had visited Morris on several occasions in Broadmoor. He had expressed much gratitude for Audrey and David's offer and on this very morning had agreed to the adoption and to no further contact during the minority of the children. There would seem therefore to be no reason why the children should not join Audrey and David at their home in Rickmansworth as soon as possible so that disruption for the children should be kept to a minimum. Also in some respects the home in Northampton was not entirely satisfactory.

It was a considerable time later, while waiting for a haircut, that David came across a report in the Daily Mail about the closure of an unsuitable children's home giving the full name of the very same Diana. He was asked the question; when could they collect the children and be ready to accommodate them and assume responsibility? The date of the following Saturday was agreed. That this was possible was due to the fact that coincidentally Audrey had already resigned and left her current job as an industrial nurse and was due to take a new post on the following Monday nearer to her home. She only needed to write to say she regretfully could not take up her new appointment. That she was more than ready to do this possibly reflected the fact that although they had been trying for children, even at this early stage in their marriage, this had not happened and it had even been investigated medically. This had resulted in what was to be proved later to be a very unlikely suggestion that it would not be possible.

Finally David asked if there could be any special support for the children. Although they would accept full responsibility in every way it would seem desirable for the children to be educated in a particularly safe and caring environment. Could there be any company funds available to help pay for the school fees at Audrey's old school where the delicate problems, which obviously could arise, could be readily explained to her old head mistress with whom she had a close relationship, having been Head Girl only 6 years previously? Mr Shade replied that in view of the delicate situation with children it would be possible for the company to be responsible for the children's school fees until they left school and undertook to provide information regarding the company's commitment at an early date. After shaking hands all that was required was to confirm the appointment for the following Saturday to pick up the children.

After returning home an intense series of preparations began. The spare single bed was moved from the spare bedroom to the small box room. Two single beds which had been used by Audrey and her sister Pamela were provided by Mary and Frederick. The spare bedroom in their semi-detached house was surprisingly large so it could double as a playroom. A small whitewood wardrobe was rapidly purchased and even more quickly painted the colour pink. Mary and Frederick provided sheets and blankets for the beds as well. After all this frantic activity, Saturday arrived all too quickly. In spite of being frantically busy, Audrey and David found that being associated with a murder, even if nobody around them knew about it, felt they had somehow joined the criminal classes. There was feeling of discomfort meeting or seeing even minor acquaintances in the street and these feelings were to last some months.

Thus it was on a cold but sunny day in December that Anne and Freda were led slowly by the hand down the gravel drive of a large house on the outskirts of Northampton. Anne aged 5 years and 9 months flounced confidently down the drive holding the hand of Audrey, while Freda who was just 4 clung shyly to David's hand as they walked slowly towards the small car parked just outside the gate. It was already clear that Anne had inherited, to some degree, the outgoing but secretive personality of her English Grandmother. This became in later life an uncanny physical appearance even though she had a horror of this because for ever after the tragedy she had associated her Grandmother with disaster. Freda on the other hand had inherited the quiet and gentler but very secretive personality of her Scottish Grandmother. Anne in later life revealed a strong dislike of Margaret so her physical resemblance was unfortunate for all concerned.

Christmas was approaching and it was agreed that Christmas day should be spent at Sydney's large house in Amersham where Sydney and Rupert would be responsible for the catering, while Audrey and David would look after and entertain the children. As a result after opening the many presents which had been left overnight in pillowcases at the foot of the children's beds and breakfast; the journey was made by car to Amersham and to Sydney's house. After arrival soft drinks and nibbles were provided and the pulling of crackers began. Clearly, the children were completely unfamiliar with crackers and were upset by sounds they made when pulled. They then refused to wear their paper hats before the copious lunch of melon, followed by roast turkey with all the traditional trimmings accompanied with roast potatoes mashed swede sprouts onions and thick gravy. This was followed by Christmas pudding and brandy butter and cream. All this was washed down with Pol Roger champagne, a favourite of Sydney's and his late wife Doris who both picked up the habit of drinking this brand of champagne due to their admiration of Winston Churchill and his liking for it.

In the afternoon, David, heavily disguised in a hastily assembled outfit with a long white beard, appeared at the front door in the shape of Father Christmas to dispense small presents from the tree. This light hearted affair was marred by the children's reluctance to participate and their extremely fearful natures. This was a feature of their early months but soon disappeared as life progressed. Finally a tired family returned to Rickmansworth and bed.

Boxing Day was spent on a similar visit to Frederick's and Mary's house on the outskirts of Amersham, which was also attended by Audrey's sister Pamela. Again a large sumptuous meal was provided which had been prepared by Mary and Frederick. This was accompanied by a pleasant German white wine and more Christmas crackers, still a cause of fear in the children who at least were persuaded to wear their paper hats. In spite of their earlier reservations Frederick and Mary could not have been kinder to their suddenly acquired grandchildren and the new family returned once again very tired to their home in Rickmansworth. The next event was an attendance at a matinee of the Windsor Theatre Pantomime which this year was Cinderella. This theatre performance had long been a feature of Sydney and Doris's annual Christmas celebrations since the ending of the Second World War. This had continued into adulthood, perhaps surprisingly after Doris's death, up until the previous year so it was almost automatically that David booked the seats before Christmas. He might have considered how the children might react bearing in mind how they had been affected by Christmas crackers had he booked after Christmas. But the thought never occurred to him or any other member of the family. In fact when it took place the performance was a disaster. The children had obviously not attended a theatrical performance previously. They found the baddies terrifying, the darkness of the auditorium was a problem, loud noises were alarming and the customary ballet scenes were agonising. Clearly there were many skeletons rattling in the cupboard. Audrey and David spent a frustrating time comforting and reassuring the children and were thoroughly relieved when the performance ended. Later, when attending performances with his recently born grandchildren, David marvelled at the behaviour of the children who have revelled in such performances from the age of 2. In the weeks that followed Audrey's old Head Mistress was visited and the situation explained; as a result the children were enrolled in the Nursery department of her old school. They started in the January term despite no written commitment regarding any funds being available by Morris's employer.

≈ 5 ≈

Bumbling Bureaucrats and Bombshells

This chapter is an account of the first months and years of the children's lives with their new young parents and the impact of the authorities over this important period. It then covers their reducing influence up to its conclusion. As David was many years later to remark; if the authorities had wished to upset, undermine, disrupt and destroy the situation and the vital relationship between the new parents and the children, they could not have done a better job. It started in the second week of January when Mr Shade telephoned to say that the Governor of Broadmoor had objected to the arrangements that had been made for the children and would oppose the adoption on behalf of Morris who had previously agreed. Clearly, Morris's agreement which had been obtained by Mr Shade must have been reluctant and this was very understandable under whatever circumstances it was made. However, the idea that the supposed rights of a convicted murderer, the author of his own misfortune, should prevail over everyone else, is completely intolerable in a civilised society. It is the result of vile politicians who worry more about the rights of terrorists, thieves, robbers, murderers and asylum seekers than the protection of upright decent innocent citizens. Such vile behaviour and opinions are storing up a fury that threatens the continuation of civilised government throughout most of the so called free world. A 'shackled world' might be a more accurate description.

Only one week later Florence Tweedle of the County Children's department telephoned to say she wished to come round and visit the house to see if the facilities of the house were adequate and the children properly cared for. When she arrived she announced that the Children's Department were very concerned about the children, their movements across the country were highly irregular and the future of the children was the responsibility of the county in which they were now living and NO ONE ELSE! These statements were delivered in an aggressive and brusque manner, almost as if it was designed to cause the greatest distress and upset.

In spite of this nonsense it was clear that the children were settling in well. They had made friends with the little boy and girl next door and were about to start school where they had already met their future teacher. They were also already attending the local church that Audrey and David had hitherto attended.

By a remarkable coincidence the church service was also attended by the County Councillor who was responsible for the Children's Department. This kind and gracious elderly lady approached Audrey and David about the sudden appearance of two children and went out of her way to enquire after the children's health and welfare, offering kind and friendly advice. Audrey and David were completely unaware of her responsibilities and innocently believed her interest was entirely that of a fellow senior member of the congregation. She was even noticed to check if the children were warmly enough dressed for their morning walk to the church. This dear lady was highly respected throughout the town and was well known for her generous service to the community and much missed when she later died.

At an early date the Tweedle stated that the Children's Department had decided that Anne and Freda should be assessed by the county's psychiatric adviser, Dr Pott. She may advise subsequent treatment if she felt the children were disturbed as a result of recent events, which of course was highly likely. Audrey and David felt they had no choice but to agree to nearly every suggestion put forward by the Children's Department with one exception. Both were adamant that adoption was essential regardless of how long this took. David was even adamant that if an eventual adoption was not obtained the children should not remain.

The objection of the Governor of Broadmoor was in the shape of a Dr Udwin who was responsible for Morris's treatment. This was made on the grounds that because he was not of sound mind he could not agree to an adoption and therefore an adoption should be disallowed regardless of his opinion or previous agreement. David will always believe that this is all part of the wicked protection by modern western society of the perpetrators of all crimes against the interests of innocent victims and society as a whole. Even since this time these rights and privileges have massively increased in England so that these rights threaten the very foundations of civilised society especially in the face of the medieval religious ravings of some members of the Muslim religion.

Of course this was an incredibly stressful time for Audrey and David. Their income had almost halved but responsibilities had doubled. The computer company had been advised of the situation and had increased his salary and temporarily delayed his move to a more stressful job. Mr Shade was dragging his feet over the provision of any school fees which were mounting with only limited means to pay for them. Anne had celebrated her sixth birthday at the end of March with a party including children's games such as pass the parcel, cutting a cake of flour and, as the day was fine and warm for the time of year, races in the garden.

Just after this happy occasion was when everyone made their greatest mistake. It is difficult to believe that the authorities could make matters worse for the children but they did, big time, as Anne would later have stated in her American way. It started with the assertion by the Tweedle that it was essential that the children knew as soon as possible exactly the circumstances that had brought them to a new Mummy and Daddy. These names had gradually changed over time from Pop and Mum to the more familiar Mummy and Daddy. This was in the teeth of opposition from Grandma Margaret who regularly visited in her Morris Minor and dragged the children back into their past. Anne was later to say she hated these visits as she associated her Grandmother with disaster. This was in spite of the fact that she was obviously the apple of her Grandmother's eye whereas Freda was little more than a pip. This was illustrated by her telling Audrey and David that Freda's birthday was the 24^th^of November. This was celebrated for several years on the wrong date before it was discovered to be 25th November when original birth certificates had to be produced for legal reasons,

With no experience of very young children Audrey and David were not well placed to resist any suggestion from the Children's Department. Only Mary with her Grandmother's experience expressed grave concern. For a number of reasons her advice was not followed and, unfortunately, Frederick did not appear to support her at all and there was no one else with whom it could be sensibly and fully discussed. So, primarily because of David and Audrey's fear of the Children's Department, Anne and Audrey were sat down and told as gently and simply as possible exactly what had happened between their parents. They were also told not to tell anyone about this which, of course, was quite ridiculous. Up to that point Mummy had gone to heaven and Daddy was ill in hospital and this should have remained the case until the children had asked the questions themselves. This ghastly mistake, which was made on the clear insistence and instructions of the Children's Department, led to all kinds of problems. Firstly there were problems at the school where other parents complained at the tales that were being told and the Headmistress also complained to Audrey and David. Secondly, and more importantly, it was David's later belief that telling this story when they were so young was to dog Anne and Freda for the rest of their lives by destroying their self-worth and emphasising a difference with the vast majority of the rest of the human race. He believes that this was probably more the cause of their later problems than even the disruption of the tragedy itself. Whereas if it had been allowed to slip into the mists of childhood it would have had much less of an effect when subsequently revealed as questions were asked by the children themselves when they became ready to receive this information..

Freda at this time was regularly attending sessions with Dr Pott having revealed some kind of disturbed nature in her initial interview whether her later tremendous appreciation of everything Audrey and David had done for her was a result of this treatment will never be known. But as an adult she forever marvelled at what they had undertaken at such a young age. Anne was declared not to be affected by the tragedy and any previous disturbances were not picked up. She was clearly already able to avoid this with her ability to deny any situation with complete conviction. This was illustrated by the fact that when told as a child not to do something that she was doing, say tapping her feet, she would deny doing this completely while continuously doing it. David later believed that this strange behaviour was caused by the fact that if her amah had complained about her behaviour Fiona and Morris had always supported her subsequent denial of the truth of the matter however ridiculous.

Audrey and David had clearly been unable to maintain their social life and visits to various friends during this traumatic period. Telephone explanations to friends had to suffice during this time. However, early in March 1964, a significant supper invitation took place. Diana an old school friend of Audrey's and Roger, who had married meantime at a ceremony that David and Audrey had been unable to attend, were living in nearby Chalfont St Peter. It was a relief to engage Rupert as a baby sitter and travel the short distance in the car and visit their house where they lived with their newly born son. During supper much time was spent in discussing Audrey and David's terrible predicament. Roger asked many questions. He was an up and coming City solicitor operating from offices in Chancery Lane. He was indignant at their treatment by both the authorities and the company. He felt the company must have funds that could be made available to help the children. After all, their father had suffered a severe illness as a result of service in stressful jobs for the company and they clearly had a responsibility. In addition, the behaviour of the authorities had been disgraceful. He would have no hesitation in taking up their case and we would discuss costs at a much later date. Thus began two years of invaluable help and advice, which cost the pittance of £22 being the fees of the Barrister consulted just before the adoption came before the court in Amersham. The rest was declared pro bono. Thus this dear friend provided the most helpful and settling help that David and Audrey so desperately needed.

Shortly after this important development, which gave much help and comfort, a suggestion was made by the Broadmoor authorities that a meeting should be held between Dr Udwin, Morris and David at Broadmoor. As a result David drove to Broadmoor on a fine spring morning and met Dr Udwin in a meeting room by the entrance to that forbidding edifice. Dr Udwin opened the meeting with the statement that Audrey and David would never ever be able to adopt the children. David protested that the whole arrangement had been made and must go ahead on that basis. Dr Udwin asked for regular reports on the children's progress and David responded that he was prepared to do this through the offices of the official solicitor or whoever was appointed by the court of protection to handle Morris's affairs but not directly. He had been made aware of the existence and function of these bodies by Roger.

Dr Udwin stated that obviously Morris would be unable to participate actively with the children since he was now officially detained at her Majesty's pleasure and would not be in the public scene. When asked by David if he could be informed when his detention ended he undertook to do so. This undertaking was never kept. Thus this unscrupulous reckless Doctor increased the anguish and danger to Audrey and David and the children. He was later to be featured critically in the gutter press for his reckless behaviour in releasing murderers who went on to commit more murders. The only positive part of the meeting came after Morris joined and stated how grateful he was that Audrey and David had taken the children. David resisted the temptation to ask for this gratitude to be accompanied by adherence to the arrangements that had been made originally. Finally he then reported on the progress of the children at home and at school. As a result of this meeting David, at 25 and Audrey, at 24, were to become involved in legal proceedings related to the adoption. This was to be a great added strain upon both of them especially bearing in mind the responsibility of the Home Office the government department for the processing of adoptions.

The introduction of a solicitor made some progress possible even if only at a snail's pace. The Children's Department gradually began to modify their approach to the adoption. The company finally made a response in the form of the astonishing revelation that they had commuted poor Morris's pension funds so that these could be applied for the childrens' benefit after certain welfare benefits for Morris himself. Thus every six months a small cheque was provided for the children's school fees. Even in the first year this did not cover the full fees and after 12 years was hardly significant. As a result when a cheque arrived with the news that Morris had been secretly released six months previously, David wrote that he felt Morris needed the money more than he did and refused further payment. There was, during this six months, a curious incident when a man fitting Morris's description was seen looking through the hedge at all the children playing in the swimming pool of the large house to which Audrey, David, Sydney and the children had moved to live in a property they had jointly acquired in Amersham.

After this time no further contact was made between either side. Anne and Freda had never asked any questions about their Father and no gratuitous information was given by Audrey or David. Finally, on the occasion of Freda's 21st birthday, Morris sadly committed suicide in Loch Ness. Some months after this date, David had been informed by letter and told the children who wanted to know the exact date. Had Dr Udwin not so foolishly opposed the adoption and written to advise of Morris's release, then perhaps the children could have been approached to ask if they would like any contact. Whether this would have been wise is another matter. Sadly the only impact Morris's decease had on the family was that David felt able to include the telephone number of the Round House in the directory, this he had removed after the meeting at Broadmoor, which had been the cause of a number of problems.

≈ 6 ≈

Salad Days

A comfortable pattern of life was established while living at the small house in Rickmansworth and this strengthened as time went by. Audrey started regularly visiting her mother and old school friends with children for tea after school. She had found the change from working difficult at first but soon settled into a steady routine. That first year the first of many happy annual holidays took place in the pleasant Dorset town of Swanage. This was suggested by David as a result of his memory of visiting during his happy boarding schooldays in Dorset. Also at that time there was a supposed superior sunshine record for this resort. It was subsequently revealed that his was primarily the result of a too favourable siting of the sunshine recorder. However there can be little doubt that the south coast weather is some of the best in the UK and of course Swanage is not too far for young children to travel from Amersham in a small car. For the first two years they stayed at the Waveney Guest House to the east of the town but as funds became easier movement to the Saxmundham Hotel took place in 1967. This Hotel had the advantage that a footpath beside the Hotel led directly down to the beach also a good selection of adjacent separate bedrooms whereas at the Waveney only one large room was used. In 1964 the four of them were together in one room. For David and Audrey it was a great relief to get away from the Tweedle and the pressures of the situation they were in. Clearly, for the children it was a very happy time and in later life Freda would hark back to this time in a curious way. Mary and Frederick came down and stayed at a nearby hotel for the second year.

Before two years of taking over the children were ended Audrey and David sold their little house in Rickmansworth and Sydney sold his larger house to the west of Amersham and a much larger house to the east of Amersham was purchased jointly. This was decided partly because of the need for support for the new young family, also it became clear there could never be a rekindling of the relationship between Sydney and the widowed Margaret, an outcome which Audrey and David desired. Perhaps because of matters in the distant past it was clear that considerable antagonism existed. In addition Sydney showed no interest whatsoever in marrying again. In this way, David was able to fulfil his mother's dying wish that he should look after his father and brother. This began 24 years of Sydney living with his sons and their families before finally dying at the age of 99 after a short illness at home in Rupert's house in February 1988.

The selection of the new house was largely given to Audrey and she selected a very large house indeed. The house was so large that even the young couple had aching legs during their first weeks of occupation due to the large distances between all the rooms. She felt a large house was required so that everyone could get away from each other if necessary. Rupert had a bedroom and stayed from time to time but his acting career kept him away for increasing lengthy periods. At the beginning, Audrey admitted to missing their little house in Rickmansworth. However, it was quite impossible to disrupt the arrangements and after a while she seemed to settle. Sydney became very useful taking the children to school and acting as a built in baby sitter. He developed a very close relationship with Freda but was never able to develop the same with Anne. In March 1965 a hearing for the adoption took place at the local family court. This was very informal before a judge, who Roger stated had a fierce reputation but who appeared very kindly, and gently asked Anne and Freda if they would like to stay living with Mummy and Daddy. They replied in the affirmative and the adoption was granted this nearly ended any further harm Dr Udwin could do. Everyone was very relieved that the initial nightmare was over. If only he had not so foolishly and arrogantly upset the initial agreement and accepted the inevitable with a degree of equanimity, much agony and damage could have been avoided.

At the beginning of life in the new house, Audrey was delighted to discover that she was pregnant. In June 1965 tiny Anita was born on a Sunday morning in the maternity wing of University College Hospital. This hospital was chosen because Audrey had trained there as a student nurse. The arrival was dramatic; at 6am Audrey woke David to say her waters had suddenly broken. He phoned the hospital who advised there was no need to hurry and that they should have a leisurely breakfast and take their time before setting out at about 10am. Fortunately, Audrey insisted they should set out almost straight away and as a result they left at about 6.45 am. It so happened they were running in a new car, a Mini Traveller, bought to provide more room for the increased family size. Accordingly, David drove very gently into London in the light early morning traffic he also believed this to be correct for his wife's delicate condition. However, Audrey became increasingly distressed during the journey. Finally, they arrived at the hospital just after 7.30 am and Audrey was rushed into the delivery room to give birth only twenty minutes later to everyone's astonishment except Audrey herself. Despite the drama and the usual breast feeding problems, which were soon overcome, all was well with both mother and baby. Everyone was delighted with Anita's arrival including Anne and Freda, who became increasingly helpful with her and her subsequent two sisters. It is very sad that Anita does not share the loving approach of her two younger sisters and has chosen to resent the fact that the adoption took place. Although obviously she suffered any disadvantages more severely than her younger siblings her attitude is distressing.

Anita was joined on the 21st May 1967 by Emma and on the 7th of October 1968 by Gay. Both births were at home in view of the other older children and were conducted by the local GP and a midwife. The final birth produced some drama as complications set in after birth but a crash team was sent for and the situation was resolved without delay or hospital attendance. These dates allowed the summer holiday to take place in the school holidays as usual, although within the holiday period the actual week selected varied from year to year. For the second year, in 1965 the five of them were in the single large room at the Waveney but after this they clearly needed to change. For the next year Audrey, ever eager to change a routine, suggested they moved to another resort. As a result Sidmouth was chosen after much discussion and a hotel selected and booked. Rupert had recently ended a period in reparatory theatre in the town and said that although he had not visited the beach, he thought it was sandy. This holiday was a complete disaster. The journey down was much longer and all the children grew restive partly because it was so hot and sunny. For the rest of the holiday it rained every day and to make matters worse the beach was shingle. An even worse feature was the hotel meals, which were served at a snail's pace. Anita was having her two year old temper tantrums and screamed the place down in frustration. It did not help that this was not a family hotel they were the only young family, all other guests were elderly and sat in rigid disapproval of such behaviour. The main activity was playing croquet on the hotel lawns in between the showers with Anita watching in her push chair. The worst day of all was when they had hoped to go to the beach but the forecast was for continuous rain. David, with his meteorological knowledge knew this would turn out to be correct and accordingly set out with their customary picnic to a woodland Iron Age fort called Blackberry Castle. The rain was so torrential it was impossible to leave the car but they were able to drive around and eat their sandwiches. The best day was on a visit to Sir Walter Raleigh's birth place and old home. This experiment was not repeated. For the next year and for subsequent years a return to Swanage took place with a stay at the Saxmundham Hotel which was a family hotel..

For a number of years Mary and Frederick came down and stayed at another nearby hotel to help with the children. In addition to the Swanage beach there were memorable excursions to Studland bay with its miles of sand dunes and in those days a very wide and sandy beach. In recent years this has considerably reduced in size as a result of erosion which is being allowed to grow unchecked as a result of the policy adopted after the purchase of the area by the National Trust. However, the gradual and safe slope into deeper water remains, as does its considerable length. Over the years other more exciting excursions took place. Exciting visits to the Tilly Whim caves once the haunt of smugglers but now closed by excessive fears for health and safety in days where children are completely out of control through lack of discipline; to the light house, manned in those days with its guided visits up the tower; to Chapmans Pool with its soft clay cliffs and its fascinating ammonites so readily available for collection by eager children. On rainy days farther away to Corfe Castle ruins from the Civil War; to the car ferry across to Sandbanks and Pool and even to Bere Regis and the humble home of T. E. Lawrence of Arabian fame. It was at the Saxmundham that the young family looked out across the bay to the anchored

Royal Yacht Britannia and sat in its garden gazing at the moon in wonder at the men who had just landed there.

Anne & Freda

Anne and Freda became increasingly settled but their progress at school was exceedingly poor. In spite of the expense of their education the children's concentration on school work was very poor as were their school reports. Also conduct at the school left a lot to be desired. Some of the wealthier parents offered home visits and excursions and seemed to provide especially caring relationships for the two children. In their teenage years like their biological mother, an interest in riding grew up. This was not allowed to become too excessive, partly on grounds of cost but regular lessons were taken at the riding stables of a school friend of Anne and Freda's which were quite close to home. As a result, much mucking out of stables and horse grooming took place with its associated health benefits. This all came to a crashing end when the young school friend was killed while taking part in a local horse show. The original head mistress had long since retired and was replaced by her deputy in whom Audrey and David had great faith. However, results did not improve and finally, when she too retired and the extraordinary decision was taken to appoint a male clergyman as head, results grew even worse and Audrey and David looked round for a solution. 'O' levels were to take place next year for Anne and progress to a sensible sixth form course seemed unlikely. Finally, a transfer was made in September 1972 to a convent grammar school in Rickmansworth transferring to the state system but which still accepted fee paying pupils. One great advantage of this school was that it had a one year sixth form secretarial course with a very high reputation. Since the girls' academic performance was so poor, this seemed to Audrey and David to be a good way to give them a good start towards making a way in life and earning their own livings. This proved subsequently to be the case.

The annual visits to Swanage continued until 1973 when the first visit to the Tenby area of south Wales took place. This was the first time that two cars had been used for the journey. This was now necessary because of the growth of the younger children. Unfortunately, before they set out Audrey felt unwell. This was subsequently to prove to be the first signs of the petit mal, which plagued her for much of the rest of her life, with periods of respite gained as a result of taking strong drugs, which had other unpleasant side effects. This holiday was in self-catering accommodation as the increasing size of the family and inflation was making staying in hotels prohibitively expensive.

It was on this holiday that poor Anne suffered from excessive sunburn as a result of lying on the beach quite early in the holiday on a very sunny day. Of all the family, she alone had become very sensitive to sun and was foolishly careless about applying sun cream when this was left to her own application. As a result she spent the rest of the holiday on the beach heavily covered up, which she didn't find much fun. Anne and Freda found the visits to welsh castles boring while the younger children were happily scampering about. They also missed the hotel breakfasts and evening meals, which they had enjoyed at the Saxmundham. They were clearly growing up and when they stopped in a hotel in Swansea for lunch on the long journey home, David and Audrey asked what they would like to drink. Instead of the usual cola both asked for snowballs, which seemed in the adults' ignorance to be harmless enough. Both were aghast to discover that in addition to lemonade with a dash of eggnog, the description given by the deceitful Anne, these contained vodka. This became the last holiday they would accompany the family as they could easily stay at home with Sydney who was glad of the company.

Some time after the family moved to the Round House Margaret herself moved to Verandah Lodge a small bungalow in a nearby village. Her visits were often fraught as she would mostly turn up unannounced; also she would turn up with some item deemed valuable from the past. These visits, while not enjoyed, were not limited. This was how Freda's real birthday was discovered when she had to produce the original birth certificates for the solicitor. One sad fact was that Margaret's two sisters, who lived together as spinsters not far away in Croxley Green, made no attempt to make contact.

The battles of the distant past and the tragedy itself seemed to provide an impenetrable barrier, which was only broken at her subsequent funeral. Her brother in Colnbrook, an old friend of Sydney's, also appeared to be estranged and in any case was soon to die. Thus she was left almost entirely alone and at her age it was not easy to meet new people and become friendly, especially with her social aspirations. She did not often invite the family to visit her at home, though occasionally they visited for tea.

In 1970 Aunt Margaret Sydney's elder sister at the age of 92 became incapable of living on her own in her comfortable small flat in Pimlico. As a result she also came to live at the Round House. She had long been David's favourite Aunt with her constant fund of stories working for famous people including the Governor General of South Africa for whom she had been cook for seven and a half years in Government Houses in Cape Town and Pretoria. She was very fond of Anne and Freda and her influence was a good one especially on Freda, who would regularly read the Daily Paper to her upstairs in her room. All the children would regularly visit her to look at her colour television as the family one in the drawing room was only black and white.

Grandma Margaret had become increasingly frail and was driving much less, so for Christmas 1973 it was decided to invite her to stay for a few days. This was rather an upheaval as a bed had to be put for her in the anteroom of the drawing room, which David used as a study when he worked at home. As bad luck would have it, a fierce gale blew up one night and rattled a climbing rose against the window pain. She woke up and screamed the house down, frightening everyone out of their wits by claiming someone was trying to get in the window. Clearly she could not be invited to stay again. For the next year she was in a not very pleasant old people's home in Uxbridge, following recovery from a stroke and she was just collected for the day. David begged her to stay there but she insisted in returning home alone where shortly afterwards she was found dead. A funeral was held in the local crematorium followed by a buffet lunch at the Round House. This was attended by her two sisters who were driven over by a friend, her nephew and a niece from Colnbrook. These people showed no interest in her two grandchildren, which everyone in the family found disgraceful. Margaret left her possessions to Anne and Freda. The family worked hard to clear Verandah Lodge and filled the lofts of the Round House with everything that could possibly be of use to Anne and Freda. Thus the tragic end of Margaret's life came to its sad conclusion. Her ashes were later interred with her husband's in Bishops Stortford churchyard.

≈ 7 ≈

Trouble Stirs

Early in 1973, Anne and Freda asked to attend a pop concert in Watford Town Hall with friends from their school and doubtless friends from the nearby boy's grammar school. After much cajoling, Audrey and David reluctantly agreed to this. The concert was attended and during it, drugs were sold openly with the programs. On the tube home they stated there was a police raid. After this Anne claimed she had found an ecstasy tablet in her pocket. This was subsequently taken one day after school. As a result, she disappeared for some hours and had no clear memory of what had happened to her or where she had been, although Bushey Park was part of her recollection. Audrey immediately took her to the Doctor's for an internal examination which was ok and to the police where she was questioned and warned. Audrey was surprised to learn that at this time one could acquire any drug one cared to name in Amersham within 10 minutes. The activity was centred at that time in the public house by the station called the Iron Horse. This was pulled down around the turn of the millennium and replaced by flats. Although missed by all cannabis smokers and other druggies, most people welcomed the removal of a source of trouble, which could not easily be controlled because of its proximity to the tube line from London. After this David insisted that any pop concerts attended would also be attended by him. The desire to attend mysteriously disappeared much to his relief.

Right from the start Anne had resented any form of discipline from adopted parents whom she clearly viewed as usurpers. Freda, on the other hand, always attempted to comply with instructions or advice even if unable to do so. She frequently said in later life that she was much happier with her new parents than she had been with her old ones. Anne on the other hand merely asked why no one else had offered to have them as if adopting parents hung on trees. She also dismissed Freda's view by stating she was too young to know anything about it.

It was around this time that Audrey found Anne had attempted to slash her wrists, although the injury was very slight, and Audrey and David felt this was only part of her constant attention seeking. She also ran away from the house disappearing to a field with a small stable about 600 yards from the Round House. Audrey became aware of this and both parents agreed to ignore it since there was little harm likely to result from this and a return resulted without any upset. There were quite enough serious problems to deal with without making mountains out of mole hills. Many years later Anne remarked that I ran away once and you never noticed. David confessed that they did know but felt that this was the best way of dealing with it as they knew where she was.

One problem which arose in these years was Sydney's horror and disapproval of Anne's conduct. It was possible that his antagonism for her grandmother might have contributed to this hostility, which he did not feel for Freda who was so different, but Anne's rudeness and insolent behaviour was an anathema to anyone who was older. Clearly Anne was the ring leader in many troublesome situations and he realised this. His was particularly aware of unsuitable behaviour when boys visited the house. The feelings between them were mutually antagonistic whereas the feelings between Freda and Sydney were of respect and affection, a situation which applied for the rest of his long life. Sydney lost no chance to report Anne's misdemeanours to Audrey when she came in from work, she had by this time started part time work because like so many modern woman she found little satisfaction in housework and home life. David had reluctantly agreed to this in spite of his complete failure to understand this modern feminist obsession. Audrey would repeat these misdemeanours to David immediately when he returned home from work adding some of her own, saying; "Guess what SHE has done today?" David subsequently regretted the series of skipperings that resulted. Though as a former prefect and head boy of a small public school, he could imagine no other way of dealing with a wilful and completely recalcitrant teenager. Both parents felt that everything they tried to do was thrown back in their faces that every standard of conduct that they had tried to develop had been rejected by Anne and the reverse deliberately selected. Freda always made valiant efforts to try to conform to any request and would always apologise when she failed to do so. Anne would never apologise under any circumstance. She would always refuse to accept any error of any kind. Her conduct in her own eyes was always perfect in every instance. Neither parent was wise enough to conclude that it had not only been Freda who needed psychological treatment, but that Anne desperately needed this too.

In the early summer of 1971, Anne and Freda had been confirmed by the Bishop of Oxford after a preparation by the rather remote and austere Vicar of the local church where they had worshipped since living at the Round House. Margaret was very pleased to attend, and David and Audrey hoped that this experience would help Anne and Freda accept and settle into a more tranquil way of life. They attended every week, if somewhat reluctantly, the youth club that was run by the vicar's son in law. It was a complete bombshell when about a year later, the son in law of this vicar telephoned with much concern in his voice to say that he had found Anne and one of the boys engaged in full sexual intercourse in the cloakroom of the hall where this club was held. Audrey immediately arranged for the pill to be provided to the girls. Attendance at the youth club immediately ceased.

Anne took her O levels in 1973 and secured the somewhat surprising results of passes in Art, Biology, English Language and Literature and Domestic Science. Both parents felt this justified the move to the new school. These however were still insufficient to secure a move to the full sixth form but a move to the one year Secretarial sixth form was guaranteed. At this point Anne declared she wanted to attend Art College in Brighton. At this time the reputation of art colleges as centres of drug use was well known and Audrey and David objected on the reasonable grounds that, if Anne could not resist the temptations of attending a pop concert in Watford Town Hall, Art College represented too great a threat. A monumental row erupted which ended with David refusing to support Anne at Art College. As a result Anne attended the Secretarial Sixth form and sometime after she left school in July 1975 she started work at a local building firm in Croxley Green. This was the result of the school's liaison with this local company. However, before this, and after a short period of temping, including at this building firm to produce funds, she decided to have some time out visiting and working on a kibbutz in Israel. She was very impressed with the organisation of the kibbutz and the way the Israeli's had created intensive productive farming out of desert. However, she was left with a lifelong horror of the Israeli treatment of the local Arabs, including using Arab farmers for shooting target practise as they tended their fields. It is beyond belief that the USA with its obsession against the benevolent British Empire has given so much unqualified support to what is the vilest colony in human history, which has been allowed to flout hundreds of UN resolutions with impunity while practising the wickedest apartheid against a quarter of its own citizens.

As each child reached the age of 16, a provisional driving licence was obtained and a course of driving lessons paid for as well as plenty of practise with both parents. As a result all five of the girls passed their driving test first time. In the autumn of 1975 Audrey was surprised to find Freda's bath water stained with blood. This was the result of a back street abortion arranged by Anne. Both parents were shattered by this and much recrimination resulted not least because of their then strongly held Christian belief that this was the murder of their first grandchild. With hindsight, it is probable that this abortion was a good thing for both of them as this was the last straw. David said to Audrey; 'I don't care what you do or how you do it but those two girls are to leave this house as soon as possible, we must remember we have three other children to protect.'

Audrey was even more anxious to end the threat to the younger children by the continued presence in the house of Anne and Freda. She found a flat owned by a local solicitor in a small house in nearby Heronsgate. It would be easy for Anne to travel to work in the first of many old crocks she had already acquired while Freda, now soon to be in her final secretarial sixth form year at school, could easily travel there by train. From the point of view of the girl's happiness, these arrangements when set up, would prove very satisfactory. Many items from Margaret's old house were transferred from the Round House lofts and taken to the new flat by David in the family estate car. Once the girls were installed there were far too many parties. Too much alcohol was drunk and too much cannabis smoked, all out of sight from the younger children and their anxious parents. Audrey and the younger girls came frequently to tea, Anne and Freda came regularly to lunch at the Round House on high days and holidays. They also regularly visited their nearby adopted grandparents. They also spent many happy, warm evenings by the ford in the valley below nearby Chenies. This beautiful spot became a source of great consolation and happy memories for the rest of their lives. Many boy friends came and went. While Anne was at last happy, Freda was clearly too young for this life style and the seeds of her later alcoholism were probably firmly planted at this time. That first year was her 'O' Level year and, as a result of all the upheavals, her results were even worse than Anne's, with passes only in English and Domestic Science. Fortunately this was enough for her to enrol in the Secretarial Sixth Form. In 1978 Freda had a new boyfriend, Michael Morgan, the son of a Rickmansworth Solicitor who had attended the boy's grammar school from where so many of their boyfriends came. She left the flat shortly after to live with him in a flat owned by his Father in Rickmansworth. Anne's friend, Alice Cooper, came to live there instead of Freda to share the costs. Anne also had a new regular boyfriend, Fred Green, who was green keeper for a local golf course in nearby Middlesex and had a tied cottage to live in. As a result Anne spent most of her time away from the flat in Heronsgate and her friend Gavin McDonald also came to live there. Both these names were added to the tenancy although Anne became the lead tenant as Freda had completely moved away. In November 1979, on her 21st birthday, Freda became engaged to Michael to the general approval of both sets of parents. In this way the lives of Anne and Freda gradually grew apart and they never lived together again although they remained close friends. Early in 1980, Freda and Michael decided to join their many friends who had moved to New Orleans in the USA. Almost all of these friends were illegal immigrants as were Freda and Michael. It was not easy to earn a living in New Orleans as an illegal but it was still easier than, in what had just become, Thatcher's Britain. Freda became employed in the famous Maple Leaf Bar and Michael set up as a small builder and also became involved in some more dubious activities. Freda did not approve of these and the relationship began to break up late in 1981. In addition, she found herself pregnant again and undertook the second of her three admitted terminations. After this David was surprised to receive an evening telephone call from Freda; 'Dad, I've broken up with Michael and want to come home but I haven't got any money'. A ticket home was immediately sent and Freda was met at Heathrow shortly afterwards. For a short time she lived back at the Round House but it was not long before she had a new boyfriend. A builder called Martin Leaf, up from Somerset, and they set up home in a Victorian villa in Chesham.

≈ 8 ≈

Goodbye to Heronsgate

While working at the building firm, Anne had been encouraged to improve her secretarial skills. Accordingly, she enrolled in the local polytechnic and in 1979 secured Royal Society of Arts intermediate qualification certificates in typing, shorthand, audio typing and communication. Both Audrey and David strongly supported her in this process. This was the time of the first conservative recession and the company suffered increasing financial difficulties and eventually Anne became redundant and started a series of temporary jobs. She had decided to live with Fred and the flat in Heronsgate was vacated for the first time and much of the household items came back to the capacious lofts of the Round House. During the lengthy periods when she was living with Fred Green, a series of late evening summer barbecues was held in the cottage garden. Fred was a skilled guitar player and folk singer so the whole family enjoyed sitting round the fire listening to his singing and playing in the growing darkness of the isolated cottage garden. Unfortunately, their relationship was always stormy and Anne admitted they used to fight like tigers. A break up was on the cards and this was precipitated when early in 1981 Anne too became pregnant and decided to go to the USA for a termination on the recommendation of Freda and at the same clinic that Freda had used. She joined her friends in New Orleans for this. Within the year she had returned, much to the chagrin of David, who felt her influence on the whole family was baleful. By coincidence, the flat in Heronsgate was still available and Anne became the lead tenant with Alice Cooper and Gavin McDonald once more. Anne had a new boyfriend Robert Dunne a curly headed builder who lodged with Freda and Martin Leaf in Chesham. She again fell pregnant and decided to return to the same clinic she had used before in the USA. This brought the tenancy of the flat in Heronsgate to its final end and more contents of the flat returned to the lofts of the Round House. Poor Freda had to return temporarily to the flat and wrap up the tenancy. Prior to the reoccupation of the flat, Mrs Roberts had refurbished the flat and its carpets and contents. This was unfortunate as the new regime without the solid presence of Freda was much less caring of the house and its contents. The end of the tenancy presented a problem and the following letters illustrate this:

To: Miss Anne Brown
The Round House
Amersham

5th April 1984

Dear Freda,

I am writing to you in Anne's absence, but of course this letter is intended as formal notice to her and I should be grateful if you would pass it on.

I write following the vacation of the flat last week. Firstly, would you please remove the settee which is in the living room? The new tenants are moving in next Wednesday and it must be gone by then. Also please remove the mattress.

I have had the opportunity of inspecting the flat and I find a considerable amount of damage and dilapidation. They are as follows:

A] The living room carpet and hall carpet have large burns caused by an iron. There would appear to be cigarette burns, one on the staircase and two in the top bedroom., therefore all these carpets would need to be replaced and I place these costs at £500.

B] The sink in the kitchen has been completely ruined, I guess by neglect in the first instance and then by harsh abrasives in an attempt to clean it. This will need to be replaced and I place the cost at £125 for labour and materials.

C] The lavatory has been allowed to deteriorate with deposits on it to such an extent that I have had to replace it. The cost of labour and materials is £85.

D] The bathroom cabinet has come off the wall and has not been fixed and the kitchen cabinet door which was not closing had come off and had not been attended to. The labour for these items I place at £25.

E] The set of cutlery for six which was on the Inventory was strangely depleted and, in fact, there were only two matching sets. I therefore have to buy a new set and i place the cost of a set of equal quality at £30.

F] For some strange reason you have taken the plugs off the television and two lamps. These will have to be replaced and I place the cost of these at £1.50.

I am holding a deposit of £300 and I should be grateful, therefore if you could let me have a cheque for £466.50, being the amount due.

Yours sincerely

Freda was very upset to receive this letter as she rather liked Mrs Roberts. After removing the items requested, she contacted David and the following reply was typed by his secretary at work on the Round House foolscap stationary. The delay in reply was caused by the delay in finding a copy of the tenancy agreement. David warned that it would be impossible to get the deposit repaid but that it should be possible in his view to dispose of Mrs Roberts further claims.

From: The Round House,
Amersham

28th April 1984

Dear Mrs Roberts,

Thank you for your letter of 5th April received on the 7th April written on Roberts Solicitors notepaper, which I was very shocked to receive.

As you know, when we said goodbye on the31st March, you asked for a forwarding address so that you could return the deposit paid by Anne. At that time I gave my parents address, and you gave absolutely no warning of the financial demands to be made in your letter. This of course is contrary to Anne's Shorthold Tenancy Agreement, which states under item 2 that she has the 'option to replace with objects of equal value all objects of furniture or household effects lost destroyed or damaged beyond repair'.

As far as your individual demands are concerned, I have the following comments to make.

A] Regarding carpet burns:

Two burns caused by an iron, one in the living room one in the hall, and three cigarette burns one in the staircase and two in the top bedroom.

To replace all the carpets for five single burns I suggest is clearly unreasonable. At the most some patching would have been required. Furthermore Anne's Shorthold Tenancy Agreement specifically excludes destruction or damage caused by accidental fire. I quote again from item 2d of the agreement' provided always that the Tenants shall be under no liability for destruction or damage caused by accidental fire'. Accordingly, your claim for £500 is not valid.

B] Sink in the kitchen:

I cannot agree that this was completely ruined. Surely it is reasonable to expect any sink to become dirty through normal every day use, and to require cleaning. Any cleaning damage, therefore, clearly represents fair wear and tear over the course of two years. I further suggest that the wear on the kitchen sink could have been avoided had a better quality stainless steel one been installed initially, instead of an enamel sink. Accordingly, the claim for £125 for labour and materials is also not valid.

C] Lavatory Deposits:

If you had provided the option, as you were legally bound to of correcting this on my sister's behalf, I would have corrected this by cleaning. Accordingly this claim is not valid.

Incidentally, I note that though your letter implies a decision to replace the toilet after the flat had been vacated, as in paragraph 3 of your letter you state, 'I have now had the opportunity of inspecting the flat, and I find a considerable amount of damage and dilapidation'. Unfortunately this is not strictly accurate, since your plumber arrived, to my great surprise, at 8.30am on Saturday 31st March, before you had the opportunity of inspecting the flat and the toilet had been replaced by 9.30am.

D] The bathroom cabinet coming off the wall, and the kitchen cabinet not closing:

This could have been attended too had the option you were legally bound to give been offered.

In addition when you visited me on the evening of 31st March, you stated that you had been having problems with the wall on which the bathroom cabinet was hung. This I take to be an admission of fair wear and tear. Accordingly I suggest the claim for £25 to be excessive and I suggest this is reduced to £13 for both of the above repairs.

E] Cutlery:

Regarding the depletion of cutlery again you should have given the option to replace.

F] Plugs:

Again you should have given Anne or her representative the option of replacing the above.

If we take claims d] at £13 E] at £30 F] at £1.50as valid claims for Anne and Gavin jointly, then the sum of £127.75 of Anne's deposit is still owing to her. I therefore request on Anne's behalf that you return this to her, care of the above address, without any further delay. Obviously in her absence in the US, I shall leave it to her judgement whether she wishes to take any further proceedings to recover this sum upon her return, if you do not feel able to comply with this reasonable request.

Finally, can I say how shocked and upset I was that you appear to have abused your position in this way, making spurious and unreasonable claims, in order to improve the quality of the property, with a consequent increase of 20% in rental, at your previous tenants expense.

However, I am glad so little work was required, that you were able to re-let the property within 10 days of our departure.

With kind regards,

Yours sincerely,

This is perhaps a slightly unfair letter, though life is not about fairness but about achieving desired results; this produced the following reply.

Roberts Solicitors,
Amersham

11th May 1984

Dear Freda,

Thank you for your letter of 28th April 1984. I am sorry you were caused shock by receiving a letter on my Company notepaper. As you may know, I carry out all my correspondence as regards the flat in that way. It was not in any way intended as a 'Solicitors letter'.

As regards asking you for a forwarding address, I asked for it not only in relation to the possible return of any deposit due to Anne, but also so that I could send on mail and in case there were any other matters which needed sorting out. This frequently happens after tenants have left a property.

Certainly, Anne's agreement gives her the option to replace with objects of equal value those lost or destroyed or damaged, but I did not for one moment consider that she would want to take that option being

3,000 miles away. In relation to the items mentioned in my letter, it is still open to her to take that option.

I refer again to the items mentioned in your letter and firstly to the carpet burns. The exclusion in the agreement as regards damage caused by accidental fire relates not to singes and burns of this nature but to the whole building catching fire. The reason she was not made responsible for that is because it is covered by my Insurance Policy and I would claim. However I am not covered for any contents damage under the policy or under any other policy. If you consider it unreasonable that the carpet should be replaced for the damage caused, what would you consider reasonable to settle this item?

As regards the sink in the kitchen, it really was completely ruined. It wasn't dirty as you suggest, but was clearly left to deteriorate to such an extent that when you were about to vacate the flat it needed a great deal of rubbing. In fact Anne's boyfriend was at the flat when I went up there; I believe on the morning prior to your departure or on the morning of your departure, he commented it had taken him hours to get it to the condition in which it was left. When the flat was let too Anne the sink was in excellent condition. Again, if you do not think the claim for £125 is reasonable, what would you think is reasonable to settle this item?

As regards the bathroom cabinet coming off the wall, you are quite right when you say that I mentioned problems with the wall on which the bathroom cabinet was hung. This had been drawn to my attention by Anne, who suggested the wall might be damp. I accept your suggestion and agree that this item should be reduced to £13 for both repairs to the wall cabinet and the bathroom cabinet.

I have not yet bought the cutlery, but ascertained the price thereof. You may replace it if you prefer. As regards the plugs, it would have been strange to have given an option, since obviously that had been removed by you or Gavin or certainly someone when you left. However I could not wait for these items to be replaced since the new tenants needed them.

I refer to the penultimate paragraph of your letter and deny that I have in any way abused my position. Frankly, I consider that at all times I acted reasonably as a Landlord, accommodated Anne when she wanted to to take Gavin into occupation with her, accommodated her again when she wanted to go to the States and have you take up occupation instead of her and generally speaking did not interfere at all with the tenants at the flat at any time unless requested so to do. As regards the increase in rent , it really is nothing to do with you, but I would say that during your previous tenancy it was well under-priced compared with other properties in Heronsgate with similar accommodation. In fact between your leaving the flat and our re-letting it, it was almost entirely redecorated.

I should be pleased to receive a reply to this letter at your convenience or, alternatively, would be more than pleased to speak to you on the telephone if you felt that we could resolve matters more quickly that way.

Yours sincerely,

David advised Freda to telephone and try to secure agreement that no money should pass between them and that the deposit should be retained in final settlement. This turned out to be the case and in this rather ignoble way, the ten years of the flat in Heronsgate came to an end. Clearly, in this dispute there was right on both sides, so it seemed reasonable to go for this solution. David felt it was very unfair of Anne to lumber Freda with the clearing up job at the flat and wondered why it was necessary for Anne to depart so precipitately. No one, apart from Freda, knew the real reason why this was required and it was assumed that this was all part of Anne's wilful and selfish behaviour.

≈ 9 ≈

Freda's Story

After returning to the Round House, Freda did not stay at there for long but she had, however, lived at the Round House long enough for her younger siblings to notice the small collection of empty Vodka bottles underneath her bed. David never noticed these as he was not in the habit of looking underneath his daughter's beds or even visiting their bedrooms. In any case they were cleared away long before he moved away from the Round House in July 1985, after returning from working in Saudi Arabia at the beginning of 1984. He had started work there in November 1982 when, as a result of the first Thatcher recession, he had been made redundant at work and there was no work in England for him. When he had left for Saudi Arabia, Sydney had gone to live with Rupert and his younger family in Saffron Walden. Rupert had by this time married an actress with a clergyman Father and had two young boys Hector and James. Meanwhile, Audrey, who was now working full time, stayed at the Round House with the three younger girls who were in school nearby. On David's return from Saudi Arabia, he and Audrey had grown apart and as a result they divorced. As part of the divorce settlement a bungalow had been purchased for her in nearby Wendover at her request. This was round the corner from the local Roman Catholic Church and the priest's house with whom she had grown close following her Catholic religious instruction and conversion.

Freda

In the meantime, Freda and Martin had set up home in the Edwardian Villa in Bellingdon Road Chesham. As a result, this house became the centre of much family activity. Freda was working as a temporary Secretary with various companies, including a well-known entertainment company, where she eventually became Secretary PA to the Managing Director and was offered permanent employment. This job was too last for a number of years and to have a considerable influence over her life. To travel to work, Freda had a series of very old bangers. David vividly remembers one day while travelling in his work along the North Orbital Road, following a car far ahead, which was the source of a trail of clouds of blue smoke. He caught up with this car, which had then stopped in Maple Cross and was astonished to find it was his daughter Freda who was sitting inside. He stopped and was soon joined by others in pushing her off the road onto the grass verge. He then gave her a lift back to Chesham where she had a dental appointment. The relationship with Martin was both short and stormy and after a fierce fight Freda left the house one night and spent several nights by the old ford at Chenies weeping and sleeping before asking David if she could return to his new house, Clayton, in Elizabeth Avenue, Little Chalfont.

Once more Freda became Mother hen to the family. However, she didn't stay long at this house as she had met a new boyfriend at her new workplace, an entertainment company. This was Roger Wilding, the Production Director at the company, who was the son of the Managing Director for whom she was working. He invited her to live with him in his bungalow at Ley Hill. After Freda had left the house, David didn't find any empty vodka bottles beneath her bed. However, he did discover over a several months that a number of bottles in his very full but little used sideboard were mysteriously very low also and some seemed to be mysteriously diluted. This especially applied to the vodka bottle, which he never ever used. He decided not to make any remark as it was possible some of these changes had happened while he was working in Saudi Arabia. Once again many enjoyable and very regular visits were made by the whole family to the bungalow in Ley Hill. One memorable event at this time was a Leicester Square film premiere held by the entertainment company for a rather daring film which the company had just released. Freda invited David as her guest, as her partner would be much occupied in the official proceedings. She stated that of all her male friends, the one she could trust most at the party afterwards was her father. Everyone very much enjoyed this happy and successful occasion. The film was a great success and turned out to be a bodice ripping lark that David found a source of much hilarity.

The new relationship with Roger was very happy and soon strengthened to such an extent that marriage was proposed. Of course, prior to the nuptials, the customary hen and stag nights took place. In Freda's case, this was to a favourite restaurant and the party included her future mother and sister in law. This was a much more select and dignified occasion than Roger's stag night. For this a small coach was hired and the party included his father and prospective father in law. They travelled to Baker Street and the School Dinners Restaurant. Here, the somewhat plain and indifferent food, in David's case Steak and chips followed by spotted dick and custard, was accompanied by entertainment of a mildly pornographic nature. Everyone consumed vast amounts of beer while the groom was subject to the slights and instructions of the Headmaster with his mortarboard and cane. The headmaster subjected the prospective groom to various tasks of a mildly pornographic nature with scantily dressed females some of whom were very attractive while others were positively grotesque. The failure to perform any task to the full satisfaction of the headmaster was followed by action from his rather over active cane. Everyone returned on the coach to Ley Hill in a highly drunken state singing rugby songs from schooldays long ago.

In February 1988, Sydney died in the second month of his hundredth year after only a fortnight's illness. A funeral was conducted in the local church where he lived by Rupert's clergyman father in law. Afterwards he was cremated in the same crematorium at Bishops Stortford where his brother Tom had been cremated. The cremation had been followed by a wake at the delightful church rooms the former premises of an ancient public house. Later his ashes were interred with those of his long dead wife Doris.

On 14 April 1988 a marriage took place at the local Registry office in Watford followed by a blessing service in the local church. This was carried out by Rupert's clergyman father in law and a reception followed in the local village hall. The catering had been organised by all female members of the whole family. David even innocently provided a swig of brandy in the wedding car approaching the church before the service stating that it would do them both good. He was still completely unaware of Freda's growing addiction to alcohol, which was to prove so harmful, combined with her refusal to eat properly on the grounds that she would become fat like her sister.

The ceremonies and wedding breakfast in the village hall were a great success. In his wedding speech David was somewhat Edwardian emphasising the importance of husbands and wives staying together. For their honeymoon the happy couple flew to the United States to see Freda after spending the first night at the Burnham Beeches Hotel. By this time she was living in Santa Fe. They stayed in the local Holiday Inn where she had found them the worse for drink on the first morning at about eight o'clock. She was somewhat scathing in her remarks in spite of this being a case of the pot calling the kettle black and ignoring the obvious effects of a disoriented time clocks resulting from the long journey. After a happy time together the couple returned to England and the bungalow in Ley Hill.

Life for the whole family now centred round this comfortable bungalow. David was in the habit of regularly coming to supper and equally regularly would chide Freda during the meal about not eating enough. Only to receive the constant reply; 'I don't want to get fat'. As someone who has a constant struggle against a tendency to put on weight, he was not able to counter this very well. Freda had brought with her from her time in Chesham, a small wirehaired Jack Russell terrier called Alfie. This little dog was a great source of fun for the whole family. Roger was in the habit of taking him for a final walk at night to the nearby pub. It was a source of great amusement that as closing time approached, Alfie would become increasingly agitated as if to say; 'Hurry up they will be closed and I will miss meeting all my friends, my ash tray of beer and selection of crisps and patting'. He was well known in the pub and in addition to visiting his friends for tit bits would sit up at the bar taking an interest in all the proceedings. Freda would not attend these visits and would appear to be very abstemious in her drinking habits, often refusing wine accompanying a meal and limiting herself to a small sherry beforehand. Though she was often to be found during the day drinking orange juice in which it was not possible to detect the inevitable vodka. At holiday times David would visit for lunch. For several years, including Bank Holiday Monday, the 29th August 1988, Freda, Roger, Alfie and David would take part in the local fun run ending up at the pub extra thirsty and ready to enjoy the complimentary roast potatoes at the bar. This was a very happy period despite any under currents not in public view. However, it was too come to an end in a sudden and unexpected way. This was the time of the second conservative recession and with the party of unemployment in power the benefits of North Sea oil and gas were being grossly misused. In addition, to the successful but unnecessary Falklands war, this was to be squandered upon unemployment benefit greatly exacerbated by a vicious attack on the working classes and both the deserving and undeserving poor. It is a national tragedy that these vicious policies were never properly reversed by the corrupt warmonger fantasist Tony Blair. Rather than being clapped out of the House of Commons this dangerous man should have been impeached for the traitor he turned out to be.

At this time the entertainment company fell upon hard times as a result of an unsuccessful investment in a new film by its Chairman. This resulted in Freda, Roger and his Father all losing their jobs on the same day. Freda and her boss were never to work again and Roger managed for many years on a succession of unsuccessful self-employment ventures until he was rescued like many others by that new labour government. Of course this meant that Freda spent much depressing and unproductive time at home when she was not employed as a temp which became increasingly infrequent.

Everyone in the family had a great shock when in 1990 she was suddenly taken to Stoke Mandeville Hospital with a complaint that was described as jaundice. After about two weeks she returned home apparently cured. It was only six months later was it revealed to David that she had discharged herself. This he would not have tolerated and the easy going Roger would have had to put his foot down had he known about it. Audrey did know but by this time there was no communication between her and David. Unfortunately six months later was much too late for any effective action to be taken. Before long a further spell in Amersham hospital became necessary. David was surprised to be told by Freda while visiting that Audrey was saying Freda was an alcoholic and Anne was a drug addict. Clearly Freda's jaundice was none other than alcohol induced liver disease and she started treatment at Kings College hospital in Brixton. David was anxious to help in any way that he could. He hit upon the idea of paying for a series of hypnotist sessions. One day he was rung up by the hypnotist and asked if Freda spoke the truth about how much she was drinking. Having recently read about the Victorian belief that women were born with lies in their mouths, he replied sadly that in his experience of five daughters and an ex-wife, he did not really believe that women spoke the truth about any matter. He much regrets not emphasizing to this man Freda's failure to eat properly.

Roger was in the habit of going on the Bordeaux Nouveau Beaujolais run with the local publican and others. This involved driving to Bordeaux and collecting many bottles of the current year's vintage at short notice as soon as it was ready. In November 1990 this coincided with one of Freda's regular visits to the hospital in London. Freda telephoned David and asked if he could go with her as she felt she should not go alone. As a result they met at the hospital just before the appointment as he had travelled up from work by car and she had travelled by train. After the afternoon appointment he took her to Claridges Hotel for tea. They had a happy time with the splendid tea of sandwiches and delicious cakes reminiscing about Aunt Margaret, who used to go there regularly, initially with her employer and later with friends, before she left London for the Round House. Both Freda and David greatly enjoyed this happy interlude feeling close to the Aunt and Great Aunt they both loved.

In the autumn of 1991 Anne, who was becoming increasingly concerned far away in the USA, decided to visit Freda at home. She flew over and stayed at David's house and he drove her around as much as he could. This was limited by the fact that he was still working. She also stayed with various friends and Freda and Roger. She naturally discussed Freda's situation and health with her friends and one of them, a catholic, recommended a nunnery in Kent, which ran a home for recovering alcoholics. As a result, Freda spent the rest of her short life at this home. This was certainly the last and greatest service which Anne performed for Freda. Roger,

David and Audrey would travel down separately at weekends at regular intervals to see her, as would Rupert and his wife Christine. At the beginning of 1993 Rupert celebrated his fiftieth birthday. So on 6th January 1993, a Sunday, David and Roger drove down together to pick up Freda and take her to a celebration lunch at Rupert's house. This was a happy and memorable occasion. Freda was speaking encouragingly about being able to return home as a result of her apparent recovery. They returned her to the nunnery and David then returned Roger to Ley Hill. Finally returning to his home exhausted but happy and looking forward to Freda's return home to Ley Hill.

Thus it was a terrible shock to David when on February 3rd he suddenly received a telephone call at his temporary work in Maidenhead from Roger to say that Freda had died early that morning after being taken to the local hospital overnight. This was a most terrible shock and everybody was devastated, especially Roger and David. Roger busied himself making arrangements for the funeral. This was arranged to be held at Rupert's local church for a number of reasons. A party of nuns was anxious to come by coach but for reasons of cost and time did not wish to travel too far. They had looked after Freda with great kindness and care and it was the least everyone could do to assist them attending the funeral. Another factor was the cost and complication of transferring a body across county boundaries. Also of course, Rupert's father in law was available to take the service. She lay in the same chapel of rest as her adopted Grandfather had done and their funeral was in the same church with the same family clergyman participating. The cremations of her natural Grandfather Tom, and adopted Grandfather Sydney had all taken place at the same crematorium. Finally her ashes were to be interred in her natural Mother's grave in nearby Bishops Stortford thus the whole process could be conducted by the same undertaker.

It had been agreed that the middle one of her three younger sister's Emma should read the lesson. David felt this was a good idea as this reunited all the bloodlines and generations of the family. He was a bit surprised it wasn't his eldest daughter Anita but in view of her unsympathetic attitude to Freda's difficulties this was understandable. Emma had a small child, Callum, at the time and Roger revealed in David's car on the way to the service that the reader had been changed to Audrey because baby Callum might cry. David was furious. Not only had he not been consulted, this change had been deliberately concealed from him until the last minute. Also he had not been asked to play any part in the service. He made it quite plain to Roger in the car that he would not tolerate this under any circumstances. This resulted in a furious dispute during which Roger smashed the courtesy mirror behind the sun visor in the front passenger seat of his car. Fortunately, Rupert and his father in law appreciated David's position so Emma read the lesson very well and the baby in the care of his Grandmother hardly cried at all. Following the service and the cremation, a very pleasant wake had been organised by Rupert and Christine in the same rooms used for Sydney's funeral. David was so grateful for this, in addition, he was not asked to make any contribution to the cost of this. Finally, a few months later, a small party gathered at the grave of her natural mother to inter her ashes in a small box in this grave. A stone was later erected at David's expense the somewhat florid words of which were chosen by Roger with David's agreement. Anne asked over the phone for the words; 'Let there be love' to be included. She did not attend, although David kept her in close touch by phone with details of everything proposed and taking place. It was Freda and Roger who had identified the position of this unmarked grave in Bishop's Stortford overflow church yard before she had become ill and David had then promised to provide a stone but this had not yet been arranged.

Before the above internment in the week after the cremation the ashes were placed in the small church near to the bungalow at Ley Hill and a memorial service was held. This was attended by a large congregation, which included all Freda's former boyfriends, members of her AA group, their many friends and many members of Rogers's family. David read a small tribute which Roger had prepared and included in this a reference to their holding hands as they walked down that Northampton driveway so many years before. Audrey and her three daughters decided not to attend. Later in the year, in June, Anita visited Rupert and his family one weekend. She complained bitterly about how she and her Mother and sisters had felt shut out of the funeral arrangements, which in view of Rupert and Christine's kindness and generosity was highly insulting. In addition of course, David had rightly left all arrangements to the grieving spouse and it was hardly appropriate for female in-laws to interfere. Since that date there has been no communication between them and Anita has gradually cut herself off more and more from the rest of the family. This is very sad for the two children she had with her partner Francois, who miss out as a result, not knowing their Uncles Aunts Cousins and Grandparents. Recently she has appeared to relent to some degree but David remains barred.

≈ 10 ≈

Anne's Story - Back in the USA

On her return to the USA, Anne found life in New Orleans very different. Many of her friends had dispersed and of course her sister was no longer living nearby. It is not surprising, therefore, that she visited her old friend from her Rickmansworth schooldays, Willy Smith, who lived with his parents in Dixon, New Mexico. Dixon was a small community of some 1,500 souls, the majority of Hispanic origin, set in the beautiful western mountains of California. She fell in love with the beauty of the area. At 6,000 feet the summers were warm and the winters cold but not severe. For some time she lived in the summerhouse in the garden of their house. This was partly possible because the climate was much drier than back home in England. She later moved to an Indian tepee and fell in love with the culture of the tiny Indian community. With this background and her artistic nature it is not surprising that when she moved the 35 miles to the nearby city of Santa Fe that she should find work in a rug store in the centre of town. This store specialised in selling specialist rugs, particularly of Indian origin, from Mexico itself. She found she was well suited to this job. Her English accent was an asset in selling to the customers visiting the store. Her secretarial training was very useful to the somewhat erratic white American owner. She also developed considerable business acumen and her artistic appreciation also was an asset. It is not surprising that, in this job she prospered, especially as she was paid to a considerable degree on commission on the sales that she made. Soon she set up in a flat with a female friend Lyn Wilson. After she had moved away to her first rented house in Santa Fe, Lyn Wilson sadly committed suicide, so once again she was depressed by a close bereavement.

Anne

She also bought herself a second hand truck so that she could visit her friends back in Dixon. Of course her hedonistic lifestyle continued. Many of her friends smoked cannabis heavily and wild parties were held where much alcohol was consumed. Like her sister she had a history of acquiring a number of old bangers although as a result of her drinking and drug taking she used to drive these on occasion at high speed resulting in more minor accidents and two arrests for drink driving offences in August 1989 and August 1991. Her secretive nature which had had concealed the elements of her disturbance from Dr Pott as a small child once more concealed many of her doings from her father David in England although communications were always inhibited by the fact that he liked to write letters which was not her medium, and because of his business life did not communicate by telephone in a chatty fashion as was all his daughters habit.

It was in the autumn of 1989 that her most serious accident occurred while returning from one such party in Dixon. She crashed the truck on a narrow mountain road and plunged into a ravine lying injured in this vehicle for more than a day and night. Eventually, she was rescued and ended up in the free national hospital as a patient with insufficient means. She said this was a horrible experience lying injured surrounded by shot drug dealers among the dregs of American society. It was the above series of accidents that first brought her to the attention of the authorities. She still had no green card and she was obviously part of the black economy with little visible means of support. On this occasion a hasty transfer was made from her much depleted NatWest bank account in Rickmansworth to pay for repairs to the truck. In 1991 she was visited by her sister Emma and her small son, Callum. They had a very enjoyable time and visited San Diego and the Californian sea side, which the little boy greatly enjoyed. This visit was to Anne's first rented house in Franklin Avenue, Santa Fe. On this visit she had stayed for a couple of months and had worked for a short period with Page Anne's best friend. She also accompanied Anne to court for her second traffic offence where she had received community service and about which she had been very worried. Emma also met Michael the man Anne was later to marry he came to stay during the visit although at that time he was based in Chicago. The first time Emma had visited was some 5 years earlier with her then boyfriend, Craig, and that was to the flat she had shared with Lyn Wilson, who they met. Emma described Lyn Wilson as a warm and artistic person, rather like Anne herself. Another visitor in these years was Gay who came with her partner Richard. They recalled afterwards that Anne had decided to hold a party for her friends to meet her youngest sister from England. In the middle of preparations for the party, Anne suddenly declared that she was ill and took to her bed leaving them with all the work required. They felt this was significant in view of her future behaviour.

While working in the rug store she obviously met a number of English customers. One such couple was the Browns, who were an elderly couple, Doris and Thomas, who had emigrated to the USA just after the war, and had set up in business and made a not inconsiderable fortune. They needed help with all their affairs and Anne was only to ready to supply her services including sexual favours for the seventy year old Thomas. This relationship continued over a number of years only fading away when her life gradually fell apart as a result of her failing health before her return to England and her frantic begging telephone calls just before. She would later point out to David that she had had a boyfriend who was older than he was. A remark which did not concern him greatly, though obviously he disapproved.

As a part of her work with the rug store, Anne made a number of visits to Mexico to buy the beautiful rugs that the Indians made, which were the main source of income and stock for the store. She had a ready eye for the designs and patterns that would sell well and she had an easy relationship with the country dwelling Indians as a result of her early life with the native African people she had known when she was very young.. She enjoyed visiting the Indians and bargaining with them. She also became aware of the powerful sheep dips that they used on sheep that had spread from the Western world at that time and were a source of illness among western farmers. In addition, the equally uncontrolled used of modern chemical dyes on the wool itself used for the rug making. To these chemicals, on occasions she later attributed her Multiple Chemical Sensitivity. She vividly recalled collapsing in the shop when a new case of rugs was opened after delivery. David afterwards attributed this to an Asthma attack which was caused by the family Asthma from which her Mother had suffered from her earliest youth and which David himself had suffered to a slight degree all his life but only diagnosed at the age of 55. She, however, adamantly refused to accept that she had Asthma, preferring the eccentric MCS diagnosis in spite of the fact that some of the more astute American Doctors asked her if there was any Asthma in the family. She always strongly denied this though it certainly was the case that Asthma ran throughout their mutual great grandfather, Aaron Emanuel's, family. Indeed, one young male cousin of Anne's generation sadly died at the age of 32 as a result of an Asthma attack.

Anne's visit to England in early 1992 caused more questions to be raised by the authorities. It became vital that she obtained a green card. One way was by marrying an American citizen. So on 10th September 1992 she married Robert Michael Werner in Santa Fe without at first telling any member of the family in England. She later claimed to David that this was a personal favour and there was no sexual relationship, especially as Michael was gay also that he was black, which was not the case. However David in a much later telephone conversation with Michael was convinced that at the very least Michael was very fond of Anne. One reason for not telling the family back in England was that her sister Freda was very ill in her nunnery home and would obviously not be able to join any visiting party to Santa Fe. David by this time was passed caring about her conduct and in any case, was as always heavily involved in his work. The marriage to

Michael and her green card status enable them both to purchase a new home. They contracted to buy a new property in March 1994. The final purchase took place in September 1994 when they moved to a new property in Avenue de Linda. Audrey back in England had helped by kindly providing part of the deposit required for this property.

Although she was devastated by Freda's untimely death, she decided she could not bear to attend the funeral. However, attending her sister Emma's wedding to her French partner Marc was a different matter. So in June 1998 she flew again to London and then travelled with her sister Gay and her partner to Bordeaux and the local village where a religious ceremony took place. The previous civil ceremony in Paris a week earlier was only attended by David and Rupert and his family. She obviously greatly enjoyed this trip and copious amounts of alcohol were consumed. She was repeatedly complaining about her Multi-Chemical Sensitivity. This is a condition largely ignored in the UK, certainly by the NHS although certain private medical centres acknowledge and treat it. Where the truth of the matter lies is difficult to ascertain, although psychological and mental health are obviously relevant. On returning to England she stayed largely with David who again drove her around as she visited friends and family. She also made business calls on behalf of the rug company on both the Harrods and Liberty department store buyers; all the while complaining that traffic pollution and various chemicals in daily life were upsetting her MCS. The cause of this complaint was at other times put down to the Californian forest fires, which had greatly affected the Santa Fe area around that time as it was down wind, and the fact that the rugs she was selling and buying on her trips to Mexico were affected by the above mentioned chemical sheep dips and dyes of a harmful chemical nature. She claimed that on the journey over she had collapsed at Chicago Airport as a result of this condition caused by the fact that the airport was being repainted. She also admitted that she had teamed up with another girl on her flights and that they had both got very drunk. Whether these two facts were interconnected cannot be established though it is quite clear that it was fortunate that her unsatisfactory green card status had come to an end, as it was obvious her conduct could make her a centre of excessive attention.

A visit to Rupert and his family was arranged and was a happy event. David suggested on the way down she visited her sister and mother's grave, which was nearby. He could never understand why she adamantly refused to do this. However, to avoid unnecessary hysteria and disputation he avoided insisting. One dispute between them did arise. She asked to visit a cafe she had frequented with school friends and her sister in Rickmansworth, so they had tea there together. She started reminiscing about their conduct during this period, reflecting enormous amusement and approval of this. David became very cross, largely because he felt if she had provided a little better example to Freda then her sister would still have been alive, though he, of course, did not say this. Her conduct and demeanour was clearly becoming more and more flaky. As her time for returning to the USA neared she became more and more emotional saying that she didn't think she would be fit enough to ever visit England again and that she could not return if her health became worse. David perhaps foolishly offered to go over and collect her. Just before her flight was called, she disappeared for a mysteriously long time to the ladies toilets. David became quite anxious that she might miss her flight but fortunately she reappeared and a fond farewell took place. During this he promised to continue to help her as much as he could while she was in America and offered again foolishly to come and collect her if she wanted to return to England.

During the next few years Anne bizarrely would ring her sisters and mother Audrey in the early hours of the morning to pour out her bizarre symptoms of MCS. These calls were not received by David as he had switched off his bedroom phone to prevent being disturbed by late night drunken calls for his student lodgers who then occupied his large house in Elizabeth Avenue, all the children having left home. Often the lodgers would not answer the phone if asleep and David, with his increasing deafness would not hear it at all. As a result Anne did not bother to phone and concentrated on calling her sisters and mother. In 2001 these calls became increasingly desperate. 'You have got to help me; I am so ill; I have lost my job; my cars have all broken down and I can't get around the city; I can't go on; I can't get proper medical help & attention; I can't pay my mortgage and my house will be repossessed & I will have nowhere to live. David started to receive calls of this nature in the more civilised daylight hours and everyone became increasingly concerned. As a result, he gradually acquired the telephone numbers of her friends and associates and held long discussions with them on how her family in England could best help her. A long term financial commitment was out of the question for anyone in the family, though David was willing and able to provide short term help of a financial nature to postpone any immediate collapse and secure an orderly completion of the trip. As a result of these calls and those with Anne herself, he gradually built up a picture of Anne's true situation. Firstly, Anne confessed to her marriage that the house belonged half to her husband who had now left her. She stated that he was willing to divorce her and let her have the proceeds of the house. A major problem she revealed was because she had not told her medical insurance company that she had received some sample from her GP of a nature that related to mental illness and had taken them but not revealed this fact to them. They had cancelled her medical insurance retrospectively and submitted a bill of 70,000 dollars for her previous year's treatment.. There was no way she could pay this or get future proper treatment.

David held long conversations with the following members of Anne's friends and associates; her GP and consultant, her best friend at work and finally her ex-husband. The conversation with Michael Werner was very significant. He admitted he still loved Anne but could no longer live with her, as her increasingly bizarre behaviour and depressive illness made this impossible. By now her commission income from her shop sales was rapidly diminishing and she was rapidly running out of money to pay her daily bills. Every call made resulted in the following advice. Do your best to convince her to return to England and her family so that you can help provide her with the care that she needs and cannot receive here in America. Of course in part this was a reflection of the romantic American view of England's socialised medicine and social care. However, David believed this advice was honestly meant and should be followed. Accordingly, he considered visiting himself and bringing Anne back home. However, for a number of reasons he began to feel this would be unwise. Firstly, this was because of his own chronic arthritis which would not respond easily to the long flights to Santa Fe. He had visions of hoists being required to lift him from the aeroplanes. In addition, Anne's approach to returning to England was equivocal and ranged in the same conversation from acceptance to a complete refusal to contemplate it. From her previous conduct he felt he would be subject to outrageous blackmail and everything from physical abuse to possible legal moves from her increasing number of debtors, let alone the unreasonable demands of Anne herself. The constant plea was; you have got to help me; I am so ill; I cannot undertake the journey; I am becoming incontinent; I desperately need money to continue here. The remarks about incontinence led to an agonising reappraisal of the possibilities. There seemed little prospect of any male being able to deal with female incontinence in public places satisfactorily and therefore one of her sisters would have to go while David provided the means and the finance. The only one who was possible to undertake this task was Gay who unlike Emma was relatively available in that she could take a short break from work and travel over at David's expense.

All this drama unfolded just before Anne's birthday in March 2001. She confessed that she had married and that her now separated husband was half owner of the house. Although he had agreed that she could sell it and have all the proceeds, time would be required to sell the house and prepare the move. Accordingly, David agreed to send some funds to give Anne breathing space as this work proceeded and sent birthday greetings on a beautiful card, picturing Buckinghamshire bluebells by the artist Gladys Crook. Inside he wrote:

Dear Anne,

I have this morning arranged for your account to be credited as discussed in our conversation of yesterday. The only difference is I have doubled the amount. This is not to pay off your debts but to give you a breathing space to sell your house and rearrange your life. As far as your illness is concerned you really do need to realise that however horrible it is you are not the only person in the world to be ill, suffer pain, or suffer tragedy Try and be more balanced in your reactions to it and in Aunt Margaret's words 'learn to live with it' There must be some things that you can do to reduce and forget the pain. You should concentrate on these and work hard reducing the pain and discomfort. I know this is not easy but like selling the house you have no alternative!

I am afraid I have come to the conclusion that it is no use my coming over. I really am too much of an invalid. I cannot sit in a plane for such hours without seizing up altogether. I simply have to be sensible and realise I cannot do what I would like to do and must keep to my gentle routine. My arthritis is really quite severe at times which is why I have moved to a bungalow.

I hope you like this painting of a Bucks bluebell wood. The bluebells are already starting in the woods although it is a few weeks yet before they bloom and whether we will be able to walk among them is uncertain as the Foot and Mouth restrictions are getting worse.

I hope you are feeling a bit better when you get this and that you are able to celebrate your birthday at least in a small way.

Lots of love,
Dad.

Eventually after much heart searching it was agreed that Gay would take a holiday and stay in a nearby hotel, hire a car and help her to pack up her house and then to return to England with her. All this at David's expense. As a not very wealthy recently retired man, this was not welcome but seemed the best solution all round. Gay later stated that she felt this whole procedure was unnecessary and that her presence was superfluous. David however felt that it was worthwhile and had assisted Anne in making the tragic brake with her American life which she had grown to love.

≈ 11 ≈

Return to England

Initially, she returned to David's home but it had always been planned that she would live temporarily with Gay and her partner in their nearby cottage, while she sought suitable rented accommodation. This was in part because David's relations with Anne had always been poor and he found her illness, which was obviously mental, extremely difficult to deal with. In addition, her raids on his well-stocked but little used drinks cupboard and her rattling around in his small bungalow late at night caused problems. He had moved to this bungalow in Amersham with its converted roof space with bedroom and adjoining bathroom in October 1999. This was approached by a space-saving, very steep staircase like that on a ship. On arrival Anne demanded that meals were served to her in bed, but there was no way he could struggle up the steep stairs with trays with his severe arthritis. In addition, he was so concerned about her night time activities that he had a bolt fitted to his bedroom door to be on the safe side. In part this was because in her lengthy descriptions of her MCS she had frequently thrown out dark hints about sufferers attacking parents who doubted facts about their illness. There was also the dark memory of her Fathers behaviour.

On arrival in England, Anne expressed great interest in attending a private hospital in Berkhamsted, which provided private services in the treatment of MCS. Accordingly, David made an appointment with the principal for an assessment to consider the possibilities of treatment at his expense. After Anne's assessment David had an interview with the principal and formed the opinion that he was a complete charlatan who was providing very expensive services purely with the intention of making excessive profits. He did however buy a number of household products which were claimed not to cause MCS symptoms. He was later astonished to find that these had never been used and eventually he used them himself!

One problem after her arrival had been setting up a bank account with her previous bank NatWest who refused to do so. David approached his own bank HSBC who were very understanding of the situation after he had explained it fully. As a result, a basic account was set up with a cheque and debit card as well as power for David to operate the account if Anne was unable through illness. This bank provided invaluable service for Anne in spite of her poor resources and mental health which had been freely admitted. After this hurdle had been overcome, Anne banked the thick chunk of dollars she had brought back with her. There was the prospect of more as the house sale had not yet reached final completion when she left due to some difficulties on behalf of the purchaser which were never fully explained. The amount outstanding was several thousand dollars and David could not understand Anne's reluctance to set about securing this in full into her account. As always this reluctance was not fully explained until much later when she explained she wanted her ex-husband to have the balance. Whether this was the final outcome or the true explanation was never revealed. Another one could have been fear of her debts pursuing her to England.

Clearly, the initial stay in Amersham was only going to be limited so as the copious boxes sent over from the USA were gradually transferred to Gay and her partner's nearby country cottage, where there was much more room. A move was then considered. This was brought about when Anne declared that David's modernised bungalow upset her MCS. The cottage was approved because, as a grade two listed property, it was constructed of ancient materials. It had also had been a second home and country retreat for a wealthy London family, the Father of which had recently died. Hence maintenance had been relatively neglected and it contained very few modern materials which were disapproved of or fresh paint work. In addition, she was claiming that her illness required her to spend more and more time in bed, which up David's stairs with his arthritis was proving increasingly difficult. As a result she moved to the cottage, meanwhile claiming she would look for rented accommodation. This very clearly did not happen David tried to take her to find a suitable property at the necessary peppercorn rent. It became clear this would not be available. He tried to obtain an alms house, which was part of a small group owned by the church. However, this was in the process of being sold off due to church cutbacks so, in spite of several of the small ancient homes being empty, it was not possible. Clearly living at the cottage could not continue indefinitely. She claimed that her increasing ill health made it impossible for her to live anywhere other than at the cottage. Clearly, her sister's care was a massive attraction. She even claimed that she could live in the damp, drafty and neglected summerhouse in the garden. She started to complain that David's odourless cream that he used on his arthritic knees was causing her massive sensitive reactions. However, when he brutally declared that he would continue to use this even if it killed her, the complaints ceased and it was never referred to again.

However, her sister's shampoos and her Mother's cosmetics were constantly complained of for the rest of her life.

The boxes of possessions gradually revealed a rapidly diminishing pile of dollars. Anne had been registered at Gay and her partner's Doctor's practice and considerable efforts were then made to secure social security for Anne. All the family thought this was the right thing to do. She had a National Insurance payment record albeit a poor one. If the State could afford to supply benefits to terrorist's, vagabonds, criminals, and asylum seekers then it could supply benefits to one of its own who had fallen on hard times because of ill health. After some delay and investigation of her sadly depleted bank account, the appropriate facilities were obtained but the problem of accommodation remained. After some 3 months Gay's partner provided a letter of removal from the ancient premises of the cottage. This was now essential as her ever growing presence was completely at odds with satisfactory relationships between any other occupants of the house. Thus the tragedy of her grandmother who, in her hours of need because of her conduct in the past, had been unable to secure the loving care she so grievously required, was to be repeated in the person of Anne. It is ironic that Anne herself viewed this same grandmother as a source of unhappiness and bad luck. She recoiled in horror at the thought of any similarity between herself and her grandmother although in truth as she aged and her personal neglect grew she became very similar even in physical appearance. The letter of removal secured the desired result and she was re-housed in a local authority homeless hostel.

Local Authority homeless hostels are not particularly pleasant places. This is not necessarily because of the facilities provided, but often arises because of the condition and behaviour of the human inhabitants. This hostel was no exception. Created in an old single storey TB Hospital, the graceful building was situated up a long drive overlooking a beautiful wide valley with beautiful woods behind. The units provided for a single person, comprising a kitchen, bed sitting room with a separate bathroom and toilet inside a small hallway. The space was not generous but would be described by the estate agents as a studio apartment. In addition, there was a communal laundry room, with all the facilities required, at no extra cost. Clearly her beautiful and spacious home in Santa Fe, with its artistic contents, would be sadly missed. It was difficult for Anne to adjust; in addition, she had come to believe she needed constant care and attention. David, with his learn to live with it philosophy, was not perhaps as sympathetic as he could have been. However Anne's reaction of taking to her bed with the curtain drawn and the window open was perhaps the worst that it could have been. One of the worst features of the hostel was the area outside in front of the building, which was used for residents and visitors parking. With the quality of cars the occupants were likely to possess it is not surprising that a considerable amount of fumes were created from the constant revving up of vehicles that were kept outside. David himself found these fumes triggered his own recently diagnosed asthma, which, with the benefit of hindsight, he had since childhood. Clearly Anne's MCS symptoms would be made much worse by this, whatever their cause. David could not understand why Anne did not make use of the surrounding countryside, especially the woods behind. She had completely lost her habit of walking in the English countryside that she had developed in her teenage years, even if this was only for the purpose of' boy scouting' as she called it. This also applied to her love of the open air, illustrated by the fact that when living in the flat she, her sister and various boyfriends had sat by the ford at Chenies on warm summer evenings with copious supplies of alcohol and other substances.

While Anne was at the Hostel David made a significant observation. As Anne remained fully clothed in bed all day her bed clothes became very dirty very quickly. Unfortunately, she was always reluctant to change them as she complained this upset her MCS. On this one occasion, after much persuasion, she and David both set to work stripping the bed. As they worked, he felt it was significant that they both simultaneously wheezed as they removed the old sheets. He had frequently tried to get Anne to admit she suffered from asthma as he did and her natural mother did before her. She steadfastly refused to accept this so treatment was never given. Similarly, she refused to accept that she suffered from any mental illness only a bad mental history because of her father. She even revealed that her doctors in the USA had asked her if there was any asthma in her family; this she vehemently denied in spite of being told by David of his own and her mother's asthma problems.

Occasionally, the occupants of the hostel would hold a summer barbecue and Anne would participate fully in these affairs, apparently totally unaffected by the smoke of the barbecue itself. After a particularly stressful visit he would frequently park the car nearby and walk his dog in the woods passing close by the back of the hostel. When he suggested to Anne herself that she took a walk in the countryside the constant reply was that the farming practises and the woods themselves upset her MCS. Indeed this became her constant cry there was rat poison under the floors of the hostel and this upset her MCS. This was also true of the fumes from the laundry room and its machines because of the use of strong detergents which infected her clothes. She accordingly asked David to do her washing in his machine at home without using any detergent. This he always did relying on a very hot wash. He realised that as he himself was not a heavy use of detergent his washing machine was comparatively detergent free. She asked for the clothes not to be dried outside as this would infect them with pollution but always to use his old very costly to use tumble dryer. On this he compromised starting off outside and finishing in the dryer and she never complained. Again because of her MCS she was not able to use the bus into the nearby town for shopping and as a result he would visit every Tuesday to go to the cash machine on her behalf and then return with her shopping. This he was very willing to do but he always refused to buy cigarettes though he did buy a single lottery ticket each week. One week she claimed that she had won a prize and, not understanding the lottery, David presented the ticket only to be told that this was not a winning ticket at all.

These weekly shopping services were provided for the rest of her life and if he was away were provided by her sister Gay. This was not very frequently as he was only away on annual golfing trips or on his blissful annual holiday in SW France to visit Emma and her husband and young family. This led to Anne dreaming of visiting Emma as well. However, she herself accepted that she would not be able to undertake the journey and anyway her passport had now expired. David did not encourage this dream as he agreed with this judgment, especially as he was appalled at the difficulties of the journey and of any return. There was also the problem that, once she discovered some outside stand-alone buildings existed in the gardens of both of the homes that they had lived in, she would demand the right to stay in this most unsuitable accommodation with associated family care services she would undoubtedly demand.

The shopping services he provided were to be of an exacting standard. Anne declared she must only eat organic food and bottled water of her approved Highland Spring brand. The six bottles a week that she drank were extremely heavy to carry. Her complaints were bitter should any other water brand be supplied if by chance the only locally approved supermarket had run out. A similar crisis occurred if the organic baked beans had run out or any other organic product. In addition vast quantities of dried pulses of organic origin were asked for every week. He did buy a single lottery ticket each week as he hoped the dream of a large win would cheer her up. However, he refused to buy more than one as he felt she could not afford any more. One week she demanded that £70 should be spent to increase her chances thereafter he always only agreed to one escaping her anger by declaring firmly that if she was unwilling to be limited to one he would refuse to buy any at all. The embargo on cigarettes was always maintained apart from when returning from abroad he would bring one bulk packet back as a present from his holiday. He did not feel this was an incentive for her to smoke, merely a help in meeting its obvious cost, which she could ill afford. On a number of occasions he discovered her smoking cannabis. He did not know how to handle this and decided to ignore it for a time. He was able to recognise the smell from his experience of living with a German student in Elizabeth Avenue. He naively believed this student to be the possessor of no more than an especially foul smelling pipe until one day he noticed the student had left his bedroom window open leading onto an insecure flat roof. While closing this he noticed an unfamiliar tobacco like substance, which had been left open in a small tin presumably to pick up moisture. This was clearly cannabis and once experienced the smell of the foul smelling pipe was unforgettable.

He became more and more convinced that Anne's MCS and mental condition was very extensively associated with previous, and possibly present, cannabis use. Accordingly, when he read in the local paper that one of the country's foremost experts on the effects of cannabis and its use, lived in Amersham and advised the local school on the subject of drug use, he got in touch by telephone and was told that cannabis use, especially when young, would cause mental illness in anyone who had a genetic disposition to mental illness. This was precisely Anne's condition. The Doctor concerned then very kindly provided a book written in English although originating in Sweden on the subject.

This was most helpful in his increasing understanding of her condition. At this time David had a great friend who lived at the bottom of the road. Pauline was very kind to Anne who used to walk down the road and visit her when they used to sit together talking and smoking in David's absence. Pauline stated that of course cannabis caused mental illness. That was why it was called 'pot' because it sent you potty. Accordingly, he then decided to bring this use to an end on the very next occasion he caught her cannabis smoking. This opportunity was not long coming and resulted in the mother and father of a row which must have been heard all over the hostel. She, of course, lied as usual and denied that she was smoking anything other than tobacco, which increased David's annoyance greatly. There can be little doubt there must have been a social services visitor on the premises and that Anne was asked to explain the row and used this as an opportunity to create a barrier between her parents and the social services. That increased in its hostility for the rest of her life. From the start of living in the hostel the social services mental health group became heavily involved in her case. One result of the move was that a change of doctor to one in Princes Risborough became necessary. Thus, the kindly doctor, who David never met, became responsible for his daughter's care. He came to view this man's care as little less than saintly, as Anne proceeded to make all their lives miserable with her ridiculous and out of control behaviour. Unfortunately, no explanation was sought from David concerning the cause of the row, which was ridiculous and very slack as usual. Both Audrey and David initially welcomed the appearance of social services on her case. However, as the relevance of their work drifted farther and farther away from her real needs, they became increasingly hostile to the repeated unfulfilled promises and ridiculous suggestions.

The year that Anne returned to England in the late summer, Callum and his older cousin, Julian, came over for a fortnight holiday at David's house using British Airway's accompanied children's service. He took them for a brief visit to Anne, and meetings with Audrey were also arranged. This coincided with the contacts that the seriously estranged couple had over Anne's move to England and future care. A series of case conferences took place between the doctors at the local mental health hospital in Aylesbury, including Social Services, and her parents. At each meeting the services of David were required as a chauffeur for Anne and, as a result, his contact with the doctors was extensive, both at these meetings and any necessary consultations. To say the least, he was not impressed and formed the view that the doctors did not know what they were talking about as usual. However, Anne got on well with her mental hospital doctors because they were largely of Negro descent. A situation that did not apply to her parents who were increasingly critical.

Initially, the main topic of discussion at these conferences was Anne's mental and physical condition and its origins. Audrey frequently recalled Anne's self-harming as a child when she would cut her hands with scissors which occurred on more than one occasion. Both parents felt their care of Anne was frequently ignored by the medical and social staff. Anne for her part always resented their being present in spite of requiring David's chauffeuring services as well as accepting his invitation to lunch at the nearby public house. This was always eagerly accepted despite its smokiness, which David found difficult for his own asthma, although Anne did not appear to suffer in any way at this stage. She clearly would have preferred him to be only a chauffeur and meal provider and she did not want Audrey to be present at the meetings at all. Gradually the discussions turned more and more to Anne's future accommodation needs. Clearly, the hostel was only a temporary solution. At the same time her parents approached their respective MP's for help on this subject. This resulted in Wycombe council offering accommodation.

In the summer of 2002 she attempted suicide seriously for the first time by storing up her morphine tablets and slashing her wrists. As a result she ended up in Stoke Mandeville Hospital. She claimed that her attendance at this hospital was a total agony because of her MCS although she showed no outward form of distress as far as her family could tell. She persisted in constantly referring to her MCS, her symptoms of red hands, which the family could not see, an inability to swallow and severe constipation, which, of course, was the result of all the painkillers and medicines she was using. Eventually, she was discharged back to the hostel.

While at the hostel, on at least three occasions, Anne disappeared only to reappear in police care in Swanage, Dorset. On these occasions she was found sliding down the less steep sandy cliffs dressed in girlish dresses, the backsides of which were worn through. In each case she stated she was attempting suicide but it is significant she did not try this on any of the much steeper chalk or limestone cliffs nearby. She had travelled down expensively by taxi but was brought back by the police after being reported missing. It was significant that this was the only time she would wear any of her many attractive dresses and not continue to wear her black jogging trousers of approved MCS material with similar black tops. After these episodes, she agreed to a stay at the mental hospital for treatment and assessment. She complained bitterly about the cosmetics utilised by her female companions stating they caused her very severe symptoms. She was definitely happier when she was put into a separate room for a short period. However, the period of voluntary admission all too soon came to an end, leaving David with the strong impression that permanent care in such an institution was the best solution for Freda's wellbeing. But the wicked closure of the nation's mental homes, so that friends of the Tory Party could take over the properties and develop them for expensive private housing, meant that long stay places were no longer available. Another bizarre suicide attempt while at the hostel near the end of her time there, was when she was found lying on the railway line at Saunderton. A train driver travelling in the other direction stopped and asked what she was doing, she replied she was committing suicide. He reported this by radio and the police came and took her to the Aylesbury mental hospital, where they scandalously released her after getting her to sign a paper absolving them of any consequences of a suicide attempt.

On the accommodation front, the offer of a small bungalow in the remote village of Bledlow, was made. The social services were very keen on this because they said the bungalow was remote and would be comparatively free of pollution and MCS causing substances. Anne furiously attacked this view stating that, as the bungalow was in a row of similar properties all heated by coal fires and with chimney's belching smoke in winter, this would not be the case. Her parents were aghast at the remoteness. How on earth would Anne manage so far from shops or civilisation with only the very infrequent bus service, which she could not use anyway because it brought on MCS attacks. In addition, Audrey would find it much more difficult to visit than even the remote hostel. David worried how he could travel there in his car in the event of winter snow. At least the hostel could be approach from both directions on main roads, which would be kept clear. Another solution was a home of multiple occupancy, which was being set up for certain cases following the recent closure of mental homes, so that difficult cases could live in the community under slight supervision relying on each other for mutual help. This, Freda strongly declared would be unsuitable, as her companions would find it difficult to understand her MCS and use unsuitable products, which she could not tolerate. Finally, there was mention of a semidetached property in Princes Risborough. David pressed strongly for this on the grounds that it was within walking distance of the Doctor and her Mother's home being close to the centre of town but in a sheltered backwater overlooking the small town. He went and looked at the properties, which were obvious as the four semi-detached homes were nearing completion. He strongly recommended one of these as the best solution. Social services disagreed on the grounds that a petrol service station was some 400 yards away and fumes from their would affect Freda. This was ironic, as this service station became Freda's main shopping destination where she bought her cigarettes, magazines and sweets, apart from the pharmacy on its way to the doctors. David was astonished to discover this when, one day, he absent mindedly forgot to get petrol and had to buy petrol at this service station with Freda already in the car, a situation he tried to avoid for obvious reasons. Freda got out of the car and went into the shop with him and was warmly greeted by all the staff with whom she was obviously on very friendly terms. All this was achieved without any untoward MCS symptoms.

It was in the autumn of 2002 that the great move to Anne's new home took place. In the days before, busy preparations were made. David bought a washer dryer and Audrey a fridge freezer. David's friend Tony fitted curtain poles which David purchased and Audrey was busy making curtains. Gay provided a second hand TV and David provided a radio. Social Services provided a double bed of suitable MCS materials and David installed a cupboard and some china from her Heronsgate days. When the move took place, David declared that this would secure a great improvement and for once everyone sang from the same hymn sheet. All to no avail, within three weeks Anne was declaring the house was upsetting her MCS due to the MBF used in its construction and of course the fresh paint. She declared the upstairs bedroom unusable and was installed downstairs in the main living room here she replaced the curtains with dreary black second hand ones she obtained from somewhere which, despite their dubious origins, were declared MCS compatible. She took to her bed dressed as usual in black jogging trousers and a black top. The new washing machine was declared a source of pollution as was the gas fired boiler. A rather dubious red curtain was also placed in the corner of the window and David mused as to what purpose this curtain could have. The washer dryer was declared a major source of problems and David arranged for the local shop that supplied it to investigate this. Of course this was nonsense but David was determined that the chore of doing her wash would not return. A letter to his local MP sent on 10/01/03 illustrates his attempts to obtain better NHS care for Ann.

Dear Member of Parliament,

Thank you for your letter of 11th December. I enclose copy of a letter of thanks sent to Wycombe Housing. Since your involvement two changes have improved Ann's condition. Firstly she has been persuaded to have daily carers, secondly she has been rehoused. For this I would wish to thank you as I am sure your involvement helped.

Thankfully this has produced an improvement which has recently been set back by ridiculous variations in her drug regime at her own direction .Once again because her fundamental health problem has not been properly addressed by the Tindal Hospital

I realise the basic problem is the evil care in the community act which short of gas chambers is the best means ever devised for eliminating the vulnerable. I am at present considering my reply to the NHS Mental health trust unsatisfactory letter while I learn how to use my newly acquired computer. I hope I can count on your full support in any future efforts I make to get proper NHS care for Ann.

I would like to take this opportunity of wishing you and your husband good wishes for the New Year.

Yours sincerely,
David Brown.

At first, Anne used to frequent the nearby public houses in the town but she was soon banned from all the nearest ones for, presumably drunken behaviour. It was noticeable that she never asked for alcohol in her weekly shopping that David continued to buy each Tuesday, apart from at Christmas, when she would ask for a quarter bottle of whiskey. David asked her what she wished to do to the small garden some of which was already laid with lawn. She asked that it should all be grassed over. After some doubt, he agreed and sowed grass seed realising that she wanted to repeat here in England the American back yard she obviously remembered from Santa Fe. In addition it would obviously be easier for him to maintain. A Flymo lawn mower was obtained but Anne complained bitterly that this machine would not pick up the grass, a fact that would interfere with her MCS. David was rather cross about this as the steep rear garden would be easier to mow with a Flymo than with a grass mower that picked up the grass. Suddenly, this mower was found mysteriously to be without a vital part so it had to be returned to the store and a larger pick up model acquired instead. Another bone of contention is the fact that on the first Tuesday David brought the shopping in through the front door. Anne angrily demanded that he brought it in by the back door because to do otherwise would upset her MCS, only to receive the firm reply that at 67 years of age, she should be shopping for him and not the other way round. He would continue to use the much shorter route to save his legs. Every Christmas, Easter and on other special occasions, David would pick her up and take her to` Gay's house for the day where she would usually over indulge in alcoholic excess. One time she arrived back home and declared she had lost her keys. David tried the back door only to find that it had been left wide open by mistake which was fortunate as the keys were then found inside.

≈ 12 ≈

Medicine and Care

Before she left the Hostel, Anne had met a local man Brian Smith who claimed to suffer from the same MCS condition. He claimed that he had been provided with specially adapted accommodation as a result of his condition and this had led to his recovery or so it was alleged. This became Anne's ideal and constant theme, so after the first few weeks in her new home, she decided that its construction was harmful and constantly agitated about new accommodation. Both Audrey and David felt the attentions of Brian Smith were extremely harmful and greatly encouraged Anne in her obsessive behaviour. David was somewhat alarmed that Brian was also permitted to attend Anne on visits to her GP, a situation that did not apply to either Audrey or himself, although initially Audrey had been permitted to join in the GP visits..

Anne continued to demand that Gay's partner should build her a purpose built home of especially approved materials. On another occasion, Anne became aware of a flat for sale in Princes Risborough that she felt would be more suitable for her condition and tried to persuade Audrey to buy it for her. Both these pipe dreams were, in any case, financially out of the question and David felt that wherever she lived something would come in through the windows or up through the floor, which would be harmful in some way or other. Such was the power of her delusions and the power of her ever increasing need for attention and the childish needs which, as an adult, she had never been able to leave behind her. David had told Anne about his visit to London with Freda and taking her to tea at Claridges and he offered to take her there for a birthday treat. Anne demurred as she said her MCS would prevent her from visiting London. This, he understood, so a visit to the Danesfield Hotel in Medmenham was arranged for tea. The building and grounds looked splendid and the tea was excellent but the visit was not a success. Anne spent all her time complaining and sneering about the surroundings and décor, which she stated was inferior to that which she was used to in the USA.

This was a frequent theme of hers, along with the fact that she should have stayed in America and not returned to England as MCS was taken seriously in America, which was not the case in England. He would also take her to a public house for lunch on days other than Tuesday, the day of his shopping trip. Anne appeared to enjoy these and did not seem affected by any smoking in the room, which was not the case as far as David was concerned. Another activity arose when Rupert stated he knew a private practitioner of cranial therapy. Anne declared this was most helpful in cases of MCS. As a result a series of trips took place down to Sussex for treatment and afterwards for tea at Rupert's home. On the way down they would stop for a pub lunch and while Anne was receiving treatment, David would walk Casey, his little dog. Sometimes he would sit in the village's pretty memorial garden where, engraved on a block, were the words of that old Victorian song that Aunt Margaret used to often quote. 'With the song of the bees for pardon and the song of the birds for mirth ones nearer Gods heart in a garden than anywhere else on earth'

These treatments took place over two summers. David felt unable to undertake the journey in the dark winter months. It was over lunch on one of these trips that Anne frankly admitted that she had hit cannabis big time while she was in the USA. They came to a sudden end with the illness of the service provider who declared she was unable to continue the treatment. The trips were a complete nightmare for David as he found Anne's smoking in the car unbearable and Anne then demanded frequent smoking stops, which greatly prolonged the journey. The procedure seemed to relieve Anne to some small extent but could not be resumed after the practitioner's prolonged illness. David and Audrey constantly tried to obtain better support for Anne with the GP and social services. David by letter and Audrey by phone. As a result, social service's care workers were engaged to cook her midday meal at her expense. They were not supposed to shop for her but some of the more kindly ones did so unofficially. At one stage a male shopping advisor appeared and wanted to take Anne shopping to teach her how to shop. She completely refused to do this and, as a result, he gave up. One day, one of the carers approached David and stated Anne had threatened her male neighbour with a knife, saying she did not believe that this was so. David regretfully assured her that he thought this was likely to be true. Later, Anne confessed that it was indeed the case and was because the neighbour had been revving up his car in the parking space in front of the two semidetached houses producing copious fumes, which entered her darkened room. She became quite friendly with the eccentric elderly lady opposite. They were both cat lovers and exchanged presents at Christmas. Apart from that, connections with her neighbours were miniscule.

Early in 2002, David began to have discussions with Julie McCavity, Anne's mental health social worker and the first matter he raised was Anne's smoking. This was because he believed that, in addition to it aggravating greatly his own

Asthma, this was a major cause of Anne's own symptoms, if there was any truth in her MCS theories, which the social workers appeared believe implicitly. Shortly afterwards, Anne declared that she hated Ms McCavity and the conversations ceased. It was some time before he was able to talk again to Ms McCavity, as she avoided answering his calls. At last, when they spoke, she declared that Anne had stated she did not wish the social workers to talk to her parents and, as a result, she was unable to do so. This of course, was a direct result of the absurd idea that the insane had rights, which needed to be respected even if it made their condition worse. This wicked idea, the result of wicked modern politics and doctor's practice, causes immense, unnecessary suffering for both the mentally ill and anyone who is responsible for them.

David, after much persuasion, secured Anne's signature on the following written statement:

I, Anne Brown, realising that discussion between mental health staff and my family is in my own interests fully agree and authorise that this should take place regarding both my diagnosis and state of mind plus any other relevant matter. This agreement should override any verbal remark made by me previously and in the future until rescinded by me in writing.

Signed
Anne Brown.
13/08/02

This was ignored and as a result he tried another tack. He wrote a letter of complaint to the Buckinghamshire Mental Health NHS Trust about the treatment and care of Anne. This was no criticism of her caring GP but an appeal in an effort to secure residential care to retrieve a deteriorating situation. The letter of complaint concluded with the following statements:

The rest of the time she communicates with a series of lies evasions and unrealistic demands with very rare moments of lucidity. She is violent with members of the family and has made so many attempts at suicide in the past year I have lost count.

When is the BMHT going to accept its responsibilities and provide her with the medically supervised accommodation she needs. We believe the Mental Health Services in Buckinghamshire are a national disgrace. Continuous medical supervision is essential as Anne is clearly incapable of taking any medicine supplied regularly or in accordance with instructions.

Yours sincerely,
David Brown

This letter was copied to the local MP who later indicated she could do nothing regarding the mental health complaints procedure. His letter of complaint received the following extraordinary reply.

Buckinghamshire Mental Health NHS Trust
Clinical Improvement Team,
4 Manor Close,
Bierton Road,
Aylesbury
Bucks. HP20 1EG.

7 Ocober 2002

Ms J McAvity
Incorrect house name
Correct address.

Dear Miss MacAvity,

Thank you for your letter of 24 September and I was sorry to hear of your concerns.

We will look into your concerns and let you have a response as soon as possible.

I enclose a copy of the trusts how to complain leaflet which I hope will provide you with useful information.

Yours sincerely,
Complaints Manager.

David was never able to understand how his name could be confused with Anne's mental health social worker. This was followed by a complete refusal to discuss or justify Anne's treatment. Apparently under our caring national mental health provisions families are not allowed to complain or seek help or assistance for their offspring. So much for the false freedom, about which this country is so unjustly proud. He even once again approached his MP to learn that nothing could be done.

He returned to his previous strategy of writing a fierce letter to the GP complaining about her care, drawing attention to her losing weight and not eating the food prepared for her. This resulted in a health visitor visiting and making regular weight checks. Everyone in the family was trying to help her. Rupert spent long hours on telephone calls and visited the family locally with his wife. He also arranged, through his local church, for the church in Princes Risborough to visit, which they then did regularly, though with her secretive ways Anne rarely reported this.

In 2002 Gay finally became pregnant with Max, the first of her three children who was born in January 2003. Anne loved the new baby. Up to this time she had regularly visited the cottage where Gay and her partner lived. On one occasion she even babysat with David. However the new arrival clearly gave her increasing anguish. One day, when Gay was changing the baby and breast feeding her new arrival, Anne exclaimed that she wished she could be cared for like that! Thus the sudden and catastrophic break in her relationship with her

Kenyan Amah following the death of Captain Tom, was revealed as a major cause of her regressive behaviour. From this time as the two other children were born, Rupert in October 2004 and Penny in August 2006, her visits became fewer. In addition, this happened because Gay and her family lived in two rented homes while the cottage was revamped and extended. This was partly due to her deteriorating condition but also an increasing depression was evident as she saw her youngest sister looking after an increasing brood while she could only remember her three abortions. Probably also seeing the care the children were given, upset her obsessive need for her own personal care and attention.

Early in 2005 her GP diagnosed gallstones which of course are extremely painful. Anne vehemently denied this and became hysterical about any hospital treatment, saying she was too unwell and too severely affected by MCS to receive hospital treatment or an operation. After this crisis receded, the matter was never referred to again, a fact that puzzled the family greatly. Although, through the fog of Anne's MCS symptoms and complaints, it was difficult to think rationally.

On July 15th 2005 David and Rupert's Mother, who had died 47 years previously, would have been one hundred years old. Rupert suggested that all the family who could manage it should meet and visit the small plot in the churchyard where she and her husband's ashes were buried. David agreed and arranged to hold a family lunch party on the appropriate Sunday. At first he tried very hard to persuade Anne to come but she stated very firmly her MCS was too severe for her to attend. Finally he accepted this. She then declared she did not wish to be cut off from the family and demanded to come. Eventually after some doubt she duly turned up with Gay and her family who picked her up. She enjoyed the lunch greatly and followed her usual pattern of drinking very little while everyone else was drinking and then drinking copious amounts of a fresh bottle of claret when everyone else was at the coffee stage. As a result she became rather drunk and knocked over her glass staining the tapestry table cloth which covers the polished surface of the dining room table; a persistent stain that remains to this day. After a short ceremony in the churchyard conducted by Rupert, every one walked to the slides and swings where the children played together happily with the help of the watching adults. Anne kept sneaking off into the bushes of the common to smoke yet another cigarette.

The care workers were supplied by a local company who, in July 2005, suddenly declared an unwillingness to provide Anne with continued support. This was on the grounds that they could not meet Anne's needs. Whether this was the result of some inappropriate behaviour on Anne's part the family never knew. Fortunately, after an anguished letter to the GP and a period of crisis, a new and rather larger and more professionally run company was engaged. This company provided a written record of care in the form of a handwritten record filled by the care workers with details of her GP, social worker and medical condition as a preface. This much more professional approach was accompanied by great kindness on the part of the workers who seemed to be of a more professional standard. Small shopping errands were gladly complied with and the service seemed to be more efficient despite the fact some of the carers came from relatively long distances. However, David was amazed to see that Anne was categorized as a non-smoker, no doubt the result of a lie on her part. The following extract from the manual under the heading structure note is of interest.

Carers; No deodorant/ aftershave, hairspray; even be careful with clothes; wear old stuff and no fabric conditioner.

Washing Up; Use soda bicarbonate and vinegar and leave to drain.

Cooking; Steam everything possible using bottled water.

At the moment Anne manages her own medication.

Jotter Notes; Client has Multi-Chemical Sensitivity and ME like symptoms causing considerable pain and distress. Client is VERY ALLERGIC to most chemicals, perfumes hair sprays, toiletries, fumes oils etc. Cannot go out or mix with people because of her reactions to chemicals in the environment.

Cannot use oven or washing machine because of the fumes generated.

Requires morphine to control pain levels. Has depression, very low self-esteem and can be very emotional.

Care Plan; In conjunction with other care company, provide daily hot meal – has to be steamed. No other care support requested by social services.

Please cook even if says not hungry, SHE CANNOT COOK if wants to eat.

A number of entries are available of the recorded visits by date. Some are printed below.

Saturday 27th 05/06; In a state weepy says she is being shunted off to the psychiatrists. Everyone says she is mad, sleeps very little, in great pain, had left lentils and mange tout yesterday cooked fish couscous and veg.

29th05/06: Angela said today her throat was closing up and at times she found it hard to breathe. She is losing weight and she is also coughing up brown phlegm. Made shopping list.

30th/05/06: Anne was upset today as, apparently, her doctor said she should see another psychiatrist. Went and did some shopping, picked up prescription, cleaned kitchen, swept floor. Cooked lamb and veg.

9th /06/06; Very stressed, ate fruit salad and steamed veg. The doctor came in. He is between a rock and a hard place, wants to help but at a loss, wants to refer her to another doctor. Anne tearful, I left.

26th/09/06; Anne not feeling well, was freezing cold & sweating when I got here. Cleaned kitchen, fridge and windows. Cooked lunch, went shopping. Said she is in a lot of pain has bruises on her arm.

3/10/06; Got medication and other things from the chemist. Her Dad brought shopping in. Unpacked it. Meat in freezer in small bags. Made two cups of tea and lunch. Swept floor and made bed.

11th/10/06; Hadn't eaten all previous meal. Cooked stew and steamed green veg. Made tea. Doctor came and sat and had a long listen to Anne.

13th/10/06; Made tea, cooked fish, fresh veg and rice. Washed up and cleaned down side. Threw out rotten veg from fridge. Anne took off for Esso Station wouldn't listen to me telling her not a good idea. Said she had herpes infection.

21st/10/06; Frequent visits to pass urine. In tears had a phone call from a fellow sufferer, cried down the phone. Cooked Fish& veg. Made Green drink and tea. Threw out stuff from the fridge. Bad day today.

Occasionally these daily reports were interspersed with Anne's own copious comments made in very bad writing and, in the main, containing a long list of painful symptoms.

27th/11/06; Made a cup of tea and green drink. Wrote cheque for milkman. Put rubbish bin out front, swept and washed floors, cleaned kitchen and washed up. Cooked lamb stew and lots of green veg, cleared out old food in fridge, made bed, wrote out shopping list, posted a letter to the doctors.

Anne added a succinct comment for once. Can't take the pain and exhaustion.

21/1106; Went to shops for meat and water, friends here from church when I got back they had bought a dinner and fed her.

28th/11/06; Went to butchers, chemist and Budgens. Made tea and green drink tea, cooked lunch, cleaned kitchen, scrubbed toilet. Anne is in a lot of pain.

29th/11/06: Very weepy, monthly payments increased by quite a bit, about £200 on premium rate, phoned office. Cooked steamed fish and veg. Made tea and green drink. Says she is sick of it all etc.

04/12/06: Prepared food, wrote shopping list. Scrubbed toilet floor, wash basin and skirting boards. Cleaned kitchen, made tea and green drink. Anne is very upset today and says she is getting worse. Doctor arrived, made bed and put dustbin out front.

The visits from the church, which were regular and almost never reported to her family, had been arranged by Uncle Rupert through his local church. Doubtless these visits relieved her dull routine and constant pain. The green drink was some kind of vitamin drink she considered beneficial.

≈ 13 ≈

Money Matters

During 2002, as David became increasingly concerned regarding Anne's conduct and sanity, he decided to review the terms of his will. Up to that date, both he and Audrey had always treated all their daughters equally. Obviously, Freda's death without issue merely led to informing their solicitors of her death. Over several meetings with his solicitor, Anne's situation and provision for her was discussed. Any sizable sum left to her would obviously affect any state provision for her and would simply lead to the State avoiding its responsibilities. The solicitor advised setting up a special trust for Anne. Both solutions would lead to a diminishing of the total sums available for the next generations of the family. As a result David concluded that he should simply remove all provision for Anne from his Will and leave it to his natural daughters to disperse as they thought able, a situation in which he was confident they would act honourably and in Anne's and the whole family's interest. He strongly advised Audrey at this time to do the same.

The solicitor then advised David to provide a letter of explanation to attach to his will to be read in conjunction with the will. The following letter was then written.

10/12/2002.

I am writing to explain why I have decided to exclude Anne as a beneficiary under my will made at this time.

Firstly Anne claims she is dying and insists everyone should believe this and behave accordingly. This letter grants her wish and if this really is the case the cost of specifying a special trust can be saved.

Secondly and similarly Anne has repeatedly made attempts at suicide. Whatever her intent clearly any one of these attempts could succeed even if in error. Again a special trust would be unnecessary.

Thirdly Anne cannot be left money without a special trust both because this would damage her benefit status and because her conduct is such that she cannot be expected to handle responsibly any inheritance.

Fourthly I am not convinced it is morally right to benefit Anne with a special trust even if it is legally right.

Fifthly Anne has cost much more money in her lifetime so far than her sisters. It is possible this situation will continue and it is not fair that her sisters and their successors should be deprived any more than is absolutely necessary. Furthermore I believe her sisters will continue to help Anne in any way that is possible and most appropriate. Hence I believe I am helping this process by not imposing a legal compulsion.

Sixthly my other daughters are choosing to produce a further generation who I wish to benefit. Anne has chosen to abort any successors.

Finally Anne's problems are directly the result of her conduct and life choices which have always been against my advice and guidance. It is too late for this pattern to change. It is this pattern that has cost me so much expense, unhappiness and stress over more than 40 years. It has also caused the family similar expense unhappiness and stress. I believe it is completely wrong for me to impose legally upon my heirs and successors the burden which I so deeply regret taking up. It is better for society to protect Anne, perhaps it always was. I do not wish for me to intrude any further upon her sense of independence and privacy.

Yours with many regrets and much sadness,
David Brown.

The above may seem harsh but its wisdom was amply illustrated by subsequent events.

It was during this period of meetings concerning Anne that Audrey and David mutually came to the same conclusion; namely, that they would not take the decision to take on Anne and Freda if they had the opportunity to live their lives over again. The stress, unhappiness and expense had become so intolerable with these latest problems that their patience and endurance were at an end. If any of Anne's attempts at suicide were successful then it would be greeted with great sadness but tinged with enormous relief. Of course these regrettable feelings resulted from struggling to deal with someone, who was fundamentally insane but steadfastly denied it and who should have been in the care of an institution, which our wicked politicians had destroyed purely to benefit the finances of their rich friends.

Early In July 2005, David, when collecting cash from the cash machine for Anne's shopping, noticed that a considerable sum had been removed in one week from her bank balance. He asked Anne about this when he returned with the shopping and a very tearful Anne stated that she had not bought anything unusual but that some cheques had been stolen from her cheque book. The following letter to her GP illustrates perfectly the fracas that ensued.

22/07/05

Dear Doctor,

I originally started to write this letter to you just after last Christmas when I noticed Anne had started smoking Cannabis again some weeks before. However, a computer breakdown interrupted printing and the smoking ceased so I postponed writing.

Anne's condition is clearly very complex and deteriorating weekly. Her Cannabis Psychosis, Paranoia and associated neuropathic pain is clearly worsening as is her depression and ME. Her increasing physical frailty in terms of weight loss and muscle mass is obvious. I also notice she is eating less and wasting more food. To compound this by upsetting her care arrangements is madness! Clearly care in the community [which I would describe as culling the community] has failed her completely. Surely there is some kind of permanent residential care she can have somewhere? What about the excellent mental care unit at Stoke Mandeville Hospital.

I am not getting any younger and Gay is not getting any less busy what with her small children and her partners office business to run, plus the upheaval of temporary accommodation. We can only over time reduce what little we can do for her ourselves. Sometime in early July a number of cheques were stolen from her without her noticing. On 13th of July I noticed a deficit in her bank balance when I drew out money for her and her shopping. We discussed this in the presence of Tom from REHAB *and the next day I visited her bank where I am mandated so that I can help her and established that cheques for £500 and £600 were paid on the 7th and 12th of July. I then helped her over the phone to report this to her bank on its 24hr emergency service. Finally after a visit to the bank I helped a hysterical Anne to fill out a bank form on Saturday morning which took 1 ½ hours after she had reported the theft to the police.*

I dread to think what would have happened had I not forgotten to return her bank card after shopping on the 4th July and my daughter similarly on 7th July.

Thank you so much for all your patient care and good work for Anne. Please let me know if I can help you in any way.

Yours sincerely,
David Brown.

As always, this letter was not acknowledged or replied to because of the lunatic importance attached to the rights of the insane to privacy, which is applied regardless of their needs. If only our evil modern society could give equal importance to needs which are, of course, much more important than the lunatic obsession with rights. The bank stopped the remaining cheques and reimbursed all the missing funds. Thus HSBC once again served Anne's needs very well. This incident occurred while Audrey was living away from the area having newly remarried.

The Tuesday following these events Anne was again in hysterics when David arrived. After some hesitation, she then tearfully confessed that she knew who had taken the cheques. Apparently she had been taken ill in the street and a black man, Stephen, had taken her home and been invited in and befriended her. The theft then took place. Quite why this naive individual had paid them into his own bank account and forging Anne's signature, he never knew and no further knowledge of the event became known to him or the family. Her hysterical reaction was increased by the visit of a policeman. By this time the police were aware of her vulnerability so she was kindly treated over this and no more about it was heard after this visit.

During May 2006 as David was preparing yet another letter to the GP, worried even more by Anne's deteriorating condition, he notice her drinking of water was becoming obviously excessive. In addition the care record shows one carer recording that she was visiting the toilet excessively to urinate. The letter implored that Anne be given permanent mental hospital accommodation and mentioned her excessive drinking of water. It was clear Anne's condition was becoming more serious. He felt the family could not continue the increasingly arduous task of providing additional care. He then again noticed a large reduction in her bank account. This time, the explanation was more innocent. Anne stated she had been paying for telephone therapy from the Berkhamsted private hospital they had visited at the start of her return to England. As her balance became dangerously low, Anne asked David for a favour. She stated a sum of dollars was left by her in his upstairs bedroom hidden inside a packet of Tampax. Fortunately he had never removed any of the items she had left behind in this room, otherwise he might well have thrown this packet away, depending on whether he noticed anything unusual about it. He forgot to check this out during the first week, so she repeated the request on Tuesday, 5th December. She was clearly rapidly running out of money, in addition, the constant government threats to reduce benefits, were a cause for concern. All problems of every kind lead Anne to increasing hysteria.

The care record for 4/12/06 states the following: 'Prepared food, wrote shopping list, scrubbed toilet floor, washbasin and skirting boards. Washed floors, hoovered down sides of cooker and got water bottles in from outside. Made tea, green drink and washed up. Anne is very upset today. She says she is getting worse. Doctor arrived, made bed. Put dustbin out front and cleaned out fridge.'

In the autumn of 2003 Audrey remarried a long term friend and moved away from the area, only to return at the beginning of 2006 when they moved to a bungalow. Obviously, while she was away, her visits to Anne reduced greatly and became very infrequent, but on her return she began to visit Anne on Sunday mornings, presumably after church..

≈ 14 ≈

The Final Chapter

In the late morning of Sunday, 10 December 2006, Audrey was surprised to find the front door of the little house in Princes Risborough lying open. She was also surprised to see the sitting room light on where Anne was normally lying in bed in the dark. That this was left on was a very unusual situation though, as usual, the curtains were closed. As she entered the room she noticed Anne's feet sticking out from the bottom of the bed. As a very experience former nurse she was not surprised to find that Anne was dead. After dialling 999 and calling the police an ambulance arrived to remove the body. She then locked up the property and gave the key to the police. Early in the afternoon, after attending the police station in High Wycombe to collect the key, she phoned David to give him the sad news and asked him to accept responsibility for clearing the house and winding up Anne's affairs. He collected the key during the following week. There was a short delay before the Coroner's office released the body and an interim death certificate was issued. To show how closely in touch with Anne's situation the mental health services were, David was astonished to receive a phone call the following Thursday asking if he had shopped on the

Tuesday for Anne and how he had found her! Care in the community is clearly fully exposed by this fact.

Despite their great sadness, David and Audrey could only feel relief that their long ordeal had now ended and they could live the rest of their lives without the constant worry and responsibility for the tragic Anne. Of course the wicked government closure of residential mental hospitals to allow their construction industry friends and supporters to make money had made matters infinitely worse than they might have been. Because they were replaced with care in the community, which scarcely existed, Anne and many others have died and will continue to die until they are reopened. Now our ever more reckless politicians are starting on the prisons where so many of the mentally ill end up. Once again the rich will be able to look after themselves and the poor and inadequate will go to the wall. Those same politicians proudly proclaim the merits of our bogus freedom. However, as the old music hall song has it, freedom is a thing that England boasts about. You are free to buy your dinner and you are free to go without. Had this situation not arisen the final tragedy might have been prevented and some sort of continuing security for all concerned provided but residential provisions created in more civilised and caring times are gone and are not to return, unless the English spring, perhaps awakening at last, produces a real democracy. In the meantime, the rich can afford their own private facilities and care and the poorer majority of the population no longer matter in the modern Britain.

The funeral took place in Amersham during the week before Christmas, 45 years after the original tragedy. The local Vicar took the service and revealed an intimate knowledge of Anne's desperate lifestyle. Emma, her partner Marc, and Callum, came over from France. David particularly appreciated this as this time of year coincided with their peak business week. Rupert and all his family attended, as did

Audrey and her new husband and some cousins, whose son had quite recently died in his early thirties as a result of an asthma attack. David's old school friend, Richard, was there, he had known Anne from childhood and was always very sympathetic regarding her recent condition. Some friends of Anne attended, including the young pharmacist who had known her from her visits to his shop when she collected her medication. The unhelpful Brian did not attend and was never heard of again, much to the family's relief. Anita and her family did not attend. Both Emma and Gay spoke very emotionally at the service.

As David walked out with his Grandson, Callum, he thanked the Vicar profusely as they led the mourners out. A small wake was held in the village hall close to Gay's cottage, which was now reoccupied. Gay was responsible for all the arrangements, which went very well.

One old school friend of Anne's came with her husband who also remembered the Heronsgate days. The husband became rather drunk and in conversation with David strongly disputed that Anne ever smoked cannabis excessively. As he had never visited her in the USA, he could hardly be in a position to know and David had to restrain himself from physically removing him from the hall. Members of the family went back to the house except for the cousins, which disappointed David but the clearing up of the hall took so long they said they had to go.

Early in the New Year, David and Gay began the sad task of clearing the contents of the house and in David's case settling the many outstanding bills. These required all the remaining contents of her much diminished bank account as well as almost all the proceeds from the dollars found in the Tampax packet and converted by David. Also, of course, the undertaker's expenses both for the cremation and for the internment of ashes at the Bishops Stortford grave. In the end the very small balance of £80 was distributed to each of his 8 grandchildren. While clearing the house many of Anne's deranged writings were found, some of these were taken by the police as evidence for her state of mind. These contained all the usual stuff; complaints about her MCS and pain, calls for help and understanding as well as expressions of not being able to continue.

Early in the spring, a coroners hearing was held at Amersham court. Rupert came up to attend alongside David. The court usher approached them and asked who they were. David explained his strange combination of cousin and Father and Rupert cousin and Uncle. The usher expressed surprise that they existed, as he claimed he did not know of their existence. Presumably, Audrey, in the stress of the moment, had forgotten to give details and David's existence had not been passed on by the police. A short private meeting was held with the coroner, attended by David, Audrey and her new husband. The main speaker at this was David, who explained the cannabis psychosis link to MCS. At the hearing the only witnesses were Audrey and a female police officer and the verdict was given as suicide while the balance of the mind was disturbed. David asked for copies of the material that had been used in court in case these shed any extra light on the facts. However, they were as described above. The hearing was also attended by Anne's cannabis supplier a middle aged lady in a wheel chair who had moved to the West Country. Otherwise only the press attended. David distributed to the press a statement regarding the failure of the NHS Mental Health Care. However this did not meet with the corrupt press agenda of the time and was never printed in any report.

Some weeks later David, Rupert and his family, Gay and her family, gathered at the graveside and interred the ashes of Anne. Each member, even the smallest boys, Max and Rupert, interred their spadesful. The wooden casket for Freda's ashes was now replaced by a cheap plastic pot. The internment was conducted by a clergyman friend of Rupert's as his father in law was now too frail to conduct this. David did not accept Rupert's suggestion of visiting the local hostelry after the short ceremony. Prior to this David Gay and the children had visited the Chenies ford, where Anne had requested to be scattered. This he did in a minimum quantity as he was aware of the watercress beds just downstream. He also strongly disapproves of the fashion for spreading ashes all over the countryside on land which is not consecrated or not in the ownership of the family concerned.

≈ 15 ≈

Two Reports

The following report was brought by Anne when she returned from the USA . It was prepared by a medical practitioner for her to present to Doctors in the UK. The first page is heavily annotated in red ink by Anne herself, but the only really coherent comment is included within the brackets below.

A brief neuro-psychological evaluation.
Patient Anne Brown
Date of Birth 31/3/1957
Date of testing 27/6/2001
Background and referral:

Anne Brown is a 44 year old woman referred for neuropsychological assessment by her neurologist. History was provided by the patient and recent medical records.

Since about September last year she has had a variety of physical complaints that she links to multiple chemical sensitivities. She first developed problems with her ears and sinuses, then in about February of this year, had stabbing pains in her left temple region and left ear and in recent weeks has developed stinging and burning all over her body. Her chest and throat feel as though they are closing up, and she has been incontinent at times when she feels the chemicals she has been exposed to are most severe. She has been extremely distressed by the worsening of her symptoms and is now unable to work and has stopped most socialising. She has been followed by ENT specialists and was seen in April by an environmental medicine specialist who diagnosed multiple chemical sensitivities. She has also seen a psychiatrist who started her on Neurontin. At this point however symptoms continue at a debilitating level and her living circumstances have worsened. She has sold her home, has no identified place to live and has run up substantial medical bills. She is considering moving back to England to be close to her family, but a visit to them in January did not go well and she has no place to live there either.

In the context of her worsening physical symptoms, she has developed memory lapses and has a deterioration of mood. When she was still working at an interior design store earlier this year, she would have periods of a half an hour or so when she would become confused [annotated when remodelling the store] irritable and forgetful. Now, these problems occur in other situations as well and sometimes last for days.

Present testing was intended to provide a description of cognitive strengths and weak areas, a diagnostic impression, and suggestions for supporting every day memory.

Medical History:

Medical records available include a letter from an environmental medicine specialist dated 19/04/01, neurological records dated 30/03/01 and 30/04/01 and associated laboratory tests records from ENT specialists from 6/00 through7/5/01 and an exposure history form completed by Anne.

On the self-report history, she noted a series of three head injuries with mild concussions and a very brief loss of consciousness [a few seconds] as a child. She also noted a past history of alcohol abuse, but she indicated she had had little to drink since August of last year[had two drinks on her birthday this March but felt worse afterwards, and has not had any alcohol since].

A 01/06/00 note from an ENT specialist indicated she was being followed for chronic allergies and pain in her left ear. She related the onset of ear pain to a scuba diving incident several years previously. She was diagnosed with COE, chronic AR changes, and inflammatory changes and the plan was to treat with Numibid, Sudafed, VoSol, and Claritin. Notes indicate that symptoms worsened over the next few months. On 11/01/01, she noted lots of pressure in her face, chronic right-sided drainage, posts nasal drainage, irritation, and inflammation, as well as Eustachian tube problem. She also had a red rash in various Areas of her body. It was noted that previous CT scans showed some mild chronic disease, but no acute disease. Allergy testing was recommended. A 07/05/01 note indicated no ENT problems that might be causing her symptoms could be seen. A question of glossopharyngeal neuralgia was raised, to be discussed with the neurologist. By that time she was taking Neurontin which was described as helping the symptoms. The possibility of referral pain clinic for nerve block was discussed.

She was seen for a neurological exam on 03/03/01 at which time she reported recurrent sinus infections, followed by discomfort in her neck about 11/00 and pain in her left ear that radiated over the face. She had developed a deep aching pain diffusely over the left side of her face, extending into the neck. Steroids had produced slight but inconsistent benefit. Dental infections were apparently considered and ruled out. She noted that her sleep had been severely disrupted and she had lost about40 lbs over a period of four or so months. She had developed severe depression and anxiety and had seen a psychiatrist who was treating her with Zoloft 25 mg and Neurontin 300-6—00 mg. She had lost her job due to inability to work. MRI's of the head and neck were ordered as well as blood tests

The brain MRI was read as normal except for a probable mucous retention cyst in the right maxillary sinus. The MRI of soft tissues in the neck showed only mild tonsillar enlargement and findings consistent with sinusitis. An ANA screen was negative, and serum B12 and folate where in the normal range. She returned to discuss testes on 30/04/01, at which time she related that she related that she felt she had some sort of toxic problem. It was recommended that she see a specialist in toxicology.

A 19/04/01report from Erica Elliott MD, an environmental medicine specialist concluded that Anne suffers from severe allergies and Multiple Chemical Sensitivity. The history of exposure to moth balls [Napthalene], through her work with rugs in a store, was noted, which was followed by sensitivities to fumes from petrochemicals and some natural scents. Tests that might help to confirm chemical sensitivity were discussed, but all were said to be expensive. No specific treatment was recommended, although it was noted that patients with this condition are generally advised to find lodging free from toxic fumes and to practice good nutrition.

Today Anne indicated that she had some tests performed for reactivity to aniline dyes and immunotoxicity, ordered by Dr Elliott, but results were not yet available.

Anne, apparently contacted Dr Raymond Singer PHD, who is a psychologist who specialises in evaluation of cognitive and emotional sequelae of toxic exposure but she has not yet seen him, as she cannot afford the fee.

In a brief telephone contact Dr Lampert noted that Anne reported mild benefit for pain symptoms from Neurontin, but most complaints continue unabated. The possibility of bipolar affective illness has been raised and discussed with her as she has a strong family history of that disorder. She currently continues on Neurontin as well as Zoloft. In her self-reported medical history Anne noted that she saw Dr Lampert because she was having suicidal thoughts because of pain and reactions, and not being able to work, and was having exhaustion, anxiety and insomnia. Today Anne denied any past history of psychiatric hospitalization, but noted that she had taken antidepressants on and off since 1993, steadily for the last three years.

PSYCHSOCIAL HISTORY:

Her early childhood was traumatic. Her Father was abusive and later murdered her Mother when Anne was about 5 ½ years old. Her Father committed suicide after release from prison In retrospect Anne attributes much of his behaviour to untreated manic depressive illness, which apparently runs in her father's family.

She was adopted at age 6 and apparently did well in school [ahead of the class no known attention deficit or learning disability] through grade school. However, her behaviour changed after puberty and she had many problems in school and at home. However she completed a 2 year course at a business college studying secretarial skills.

She has been in the USA, in New Mexico for about 20 years, but is not a US citizen. She has been employed for the past 8 years, with a two year break, by Santa Fe interiors. In January of this year the store was remodelled and she began to have violent attacks which she relates to the paint and plastering. However she was having milder attacks before then, Beginning about last fall, and has wondered if this might not be related to her handling of rugs from Mexico, where aniline dyes are used and also moth balls,. An 4/05/01 letter from the manager of the store noted that she began to suffer what seemed like severe allergic reactions during the last year, but showed no signs of serious illness before that.. The letter also noted that she had major reactions while the store was being remodelled [stabbing pains, burning sensations, severe headaches, irritable, forgetful, trembling week, cognitive abilities changed radically] which was unusual for Anne as she was very competent.

Anne has been living alone in her own home, which she has now sold and must vacate by [h] July20th. She would prefer to stay in New Mexico but has no place to live and cannot work due to her worsening condition. She is considering moving back to England to live in a cabin on her adoptive parents place. However she says reports that her family feels that she is psychiatrically ill based on her behaviour when she stayed with them in January. Anne also noted that the diagnosis of multiple chemical sensitivities is not recognized by the medical system in Great Britain and she believes her family will want her to be psychiatrically hospitalized if she returns there.

In her self-reported medical history Anne noted that she has usually been very sociable but in recent weeks, has become isolated, and her friends feel that her medical complaints are psychiatrically based. She has become less physically active [formerly walked, exercised etc.].

BEHAVOURAL OBSERVATIONS AND INTERVIEW IMPRESSIONS;

She was alert, adequately groomed and cooperative with the interview and testing. Eye contact was good.

Speech was fluent and informative, and she was able to give a detailed history. Comprehension of questions and instructions was intact.

Mood was anxious, and she volunteered that she has been depressed due to her worsening medical symptoms and socioeconomic circumstances. She was preoccupied with her symptoms throughout the interview. However she denied blatant symptoms of mania such as expansive mood excess energy, sprees etc. Although not actively suicidal she has thought of suicide for several months as she has not yet found any clear course of treatment for her worsening physical symptoms.

She volunteered that her family and some friends think that her problems are blown out of proportion and are due to psychiatric illness. She has discussed the possibility that this might be bipolar disorder with Dr Lampert, but this diagnosis has apparently not been made as yet.

She worked with good effect on the cognitive tests but near the end of the session, she appeared to be having more difficulty sustaining her mental effort. She was competitive with herself none the less and it is my opinion that results provide a valid picture of her current cognitive function.

TESTS ADMINERISTERED;

Wechler Adult Intelligence Scale III {WAIS_III} {SELECTED SUBTESTS}
California Verbal Learning Test {CVLT}
Rey- Osterrieth Complex Figure
Controlled Oral Word Associations
Trail Making Test
Psychological Diagnostic Interview

Dr Erica Elliott also provided the following.

12th July 2001

TO WHOM IT MAY CONCERN

MS Anne Brown is a patient I have seen in consultation for evaluation of multiple problems consistant with Multiple Chemical Sensitivity, anxiety, and depression. Ms Brown's health took a drastic turn for worse after working in the rug business. She worked with rugs that had been treated with moth balls {naphthalene] and analine dyes. Some people are more susceptible to the toxic effects of chemicals than others. Since her naphthalene exposure she has become extremely sensitive to the fumes from petrochemicals and even some natural scents. With this sensitivity she has developed an array of disabling medical problems including cognitive disfunction, chronic sinusitis, insomnia, burning and stabbing neuralgia and myalgias, deep fatigue and exacerbation of her underlying psychiatric problems.

Although Ms Brown is operating under severe financial strain, she has managed to afford limited testing, the results of which support her diagnosis. Extensive immune function testing revealed several immune system abnormalities, including antibodies to her myelin sheath. This autoimmune disease would help partially to explain some of her neurological symptoms. In addition Ms Brown's test results show heavy metal toxicity from mercury, arsenic and uranium. In addition she shows a current infection with HHV-6, a virus that has been implicated in immune dysfunction.

My recommendations are the following;

1) A full medical work-up in England with a physician who is trained in neurotoxicity and multiple chemical sensitivities..

2) It is urgent that Ms Brown be provided with a non-toxic place to live that is relatively free of scents derived from petrochemicals and from mould.

3) Ms Brown needs to follow a special nutritional program which includes organically grown foods, high protein, and high fresh vegetable diet.

4) I urge you not to minimize Ms Browns serious medical condition and to avoid the temptation to attribute all her symptoms to her underlying psychiatric condition.

5) It is my wish that Ms Brown will receive the care she needs so that her suffering can be alleviated and so that her health can be restored.

Sincerely,
Erica Elliott. MD.

≈ 16 ≈

Epilogue

This book is written without any intention of profit or aggrandisement on the part of the author. Its sole object is to try to secure an improvement in the care and treatment of similar cases. It is inevitable tragedies will occur in the rich pattern of human life and that children will be harmed and impacted by them. However, these situations do not need to be grossly exacerbated by crass actions on the part of the authorities responsible. In addition, it is hoped that our putrid politicians will at last start considering the welfare of the poor and vulnerable in the British Isles in preference to the poor and vulnerable from everywhere else in the world. Presently they believe in protecting the rich inside the country and only helping the poor and vulnerable if they are outside the British Isles. It will take a revolution for this ever to change. Could the recent exposures of corruption in our national life be the beginnings of that revolution? I hope so.

Finally, if there is a bias against the corrupt, manipulated, enslaved, undemocratic political system we have inherited, then it is explained by the fact that David Brown, the author, was irradiated by the British government during his National Service while taking meteorological observations for the

Christmas Island hydrogen bomb tests. Winston Churchill, our last honest and wise Prime Minister, said that it was necessary to test how troops would react to involvement in nuclear war. British Nuclear Veterans agree and are proud to have participated in this. They only resent all his corrupt dishonest successors who have falsely denied they were harmed. They denied that participation in such tests has been in any way harmful and in so doing prevented the medical profession in the NHS from accepting and treating them properly, being almost alone among the nuclear powers.